# When You're All Out Of Noodles

*and other parables on the lessons of life*

# Ken Jones

# When You're All Out Of Noodles

## and other parables on the lessons of life

**THOMAS NELSON PUBLISHERS**
Nashville

Published in Nashville, Tennessee, by Thomas Nelson, Inc., Publishers, and distributed in Canada by Word Communications, Ltd., Richmond, British Columbia, and in the United Kingdom by Word (UK), Ltd., Milton Keynes, England.

Unless otherwise noted, Scripture quotations are from the NEW KING JAMES VERSION of the Bible. Copyright © 1979, 1980, 1982, Thomas Nelson, Inc., Publishers.

Scripture quotations noted NIV are taken from the HOLY BIBLE, NEW INTERNATIONAL VERSION ©. Copyright © 1973, 1978, 1984 by International Bible Society. Used by permission of Zondervan Bible Publishing House. All rights reserved.

The "NIV" and "New International Version" trademarks are registered in the United States Patent and Trademark Office by International Bible Society. Used by permission of Zondervan Bible Publishing House. All rights reserved.

The "NIV" trademarks are registered in the United States Patent and Trademark Office by the permission of International Bible Society.

**Library of Congress Cataloging-in-Publication Data**

Jones, Ken, 1946-
   When you're all out of noodles / Ken Jones.
     p. cm.
   ISBN 0-8407-4140-5 (pbk.)1. Meditations. I. Title.
   BV4832.2.J6453 1993                       93-18745
                                            CIP

Printed in the United States of America
1 2 3 4 5 6 7 — 98 97 96 95 94 93

To Marcus, Nathan, and Simeon
I am blessed to call you my sons.

# Acknowledgments

Thank you . . .

Randee, Marcus, Nathan, and Simeon: The four of you, each in your own way, make my life rich. Next to Jesus, I love you best.

Ben and Judy Allen: One of the scariest things I've ever done is hand you my unedited manuscript and ask you to read it and comment. One of the bravest things you've ever done is to agree to do it. Thank you, dear friends.

Doug and Debbie Wesson and Gary and Connie Miller: You may not know it, but the weekend we all spent at the cabin laughing and talking and caring for each other helped me jump-start this project. You are a balm to my life, and I love you all.

All the people whose stories I've told in this book: My life has been changed and enriched and encouraged because I have known you. My prayer is that God will be honored by the telling of these stories.

# Contents

Introduction

1. And It Came to Pass . . . But It Didn't
   Come to Stay . . . . . . . . . . . . . . . . . . . . 1
2. It . . . . . . . . . . . . . . . . . . . . . . . . . 7
3. The Swimming Pool . . . . . . . . . . . . 13
4. When You're All Out of Noodles . . . . . . 19
5. Ambient Noise . . . . . . . . . . . . . . . 27
6. Known Only to God . . . . . . . . . . . . 31
7. Original Joe's . . . . . . . . . . . . . . . . 36
8. Idol Words . . . . . . . . . . . . . . . . . 41
9. The Smells of Thanksgiving . . . . . . . . 44
10. Mrs. Berryman's Song . . . . . . . . . . . 51
11. The Violence of Life . . . . . . . . . . . . 57
12. The Key of A . . . . . . . . . . . . . . . . 64
13. The Mourning After . . . . . . . . . . . . 69
14. Junior High Chapel . . . . . . . . . . . . 77
15. Bandit . . . . . . . . . . . . . . . . . . . 87
16. They Say San Diego Is Lovely
    This Time of Year . . . . . . . . . . . . . 93

17. The Apartment . . . . . . . . . . . . . . . . 98

18. I Bumped into the Door . . . . . . . . . . 104

19. The Christmas Card . . . . . . . . . . 108

20. The Duffel Bag . . . . . . . . . . . . . . . 113

21. In a Minute . . . . . . . . . . . . . . . . 118

22. I Hate It When That Happens . . . . . . . 123

23. Benjamin . . . . . . . . . . . . . . . . . 128

24. Jacob's Well . . . . . . . . . . . . . . . . 134

25. The White House . . . . . . . . . . . . . 140

26. Whose Turn Is It, Anyway? . . . . . . . . 145

27. Orange Suds . . . . . . . . . . . . . . 150

28. Memo to a Mugger . . . . . . . . . . . . 157

29. Yesterday . . . . . . . . . . . . . . . . 163

30. On Days When There Are No Words . . . . 170

31. The Peace of Paper . . . . . . . . . . . . 175

32. The Masked Man . . . . . . . . . . . . . 179

33. The Retreat . . . . . . . . . . . . . . . 184

About the Author . . . . . . . . . . . . . . . . 191

# Introduction

God is very wise. When He decided it was time for "time" to begin, He divided life into bite-sized pieces—seconds and minutes, moments for living—each identical in length to all the others, yet each totally unique.

And He strung them together in a line.

When the line was sixty minutes long, He tied a knot and said, "Enough. Sixty minutes are long enough for every hour." And He began to measure again. Another sixty minutes; another hour; another knot.

Twenty-four times God measured, and tied; and there was evening, and there was morning, before He stopped and called it a day.

The very wise God tied one day to the next until He had wrapped up a seven-day week, each with its own beginning and ending, each with its own measure of grace and provision and light.

And He said, "This is good."

Since the very beginning, it has been so. The Infinite Creator has set into motion a parade of days, each one following the other, each one filled with unexpected, unannounced events. Even though every day is the same length, no two are ever alike.

Some days are filled with difficulties and challenges that are so overwhelming it seems as though they will never end.

But they do.

Some days are filled with so much happiness and delight that we *hope* they will never end.

But they do.

Life passes through, a day at a time, like some transient on his way to parts unknown; like a traveler who happens by, stopping for a drink of water and a bite of food at some nameless wide spot in the road before continuing his trek.

Disappointments and failures. Victories and triumphs. They're all a part of life. Each day holds its own mysteries; knots that get tangled; joys and challenges and sorrows that Jesus wants to help us sort out.

I hope you will be encouraged by reading this little book; encouraged to look to God every day in faith; encouraged on days when there are no words to describe how you feel. And I pray these stories will help remind you of the transitory nature of life.

Experience it; taste it; try to understand it.

But don't get too familiar with it, because life's a lot like the manna of old. Each moment will have its own measure of grace and provision and light . . . but each can only be gathered one day at a time.

Kj

# ◆1◆

# And It Came to Pass . . .
# But It Didn't Come to Stay

I will tell you a story about a man who was forever losing things. He was a good man; a decent man who often misplaced things.

He lost the keys to his car about once a week. His wife tried to help him with his problem by putting up a key rack near the front door of their home, so that when he walked in he could hang up his keys. But the man struggled with the habit of hanging up keys, and so he laid them on the piano, or tossed them on the desk, or set them on the mantle . . . and he lost his keys about once a week.

It didn't bother him too much to lose his keys. When he couldn't find them, he'd just stop for a moment and think about the last place he remembered having them.

Then, he would go back to that spot, and there he would find them.

Losing things became a way of life for the man. He lost pocketknives. He lost expensive pens. After awhile, he just sort of *expected* to lose things.

He came to understand that much of life was comprised of *losings* and *findings*, and that it didn't pay to get too concerned when you lost things like keys or pocketknives or pens. Sooner or later, they'd turn up.

And so he went along in life not worrying too much about what he lost, and what he didn't. Maybe that was part of his problem.

For it came to pass—last week—that he lost something very, very important. He knew *where* he lost it. He lost it in the kitchen, right next to the white pantry door.

He knew *when* he lost it. It was Tuesday evening, about eight-thirty.

He knew what he was *doing* when he lost it. He was standing in the kitchen next to the white pantry door reading a note he had written to his teenage son early that morning:

*Simeon,*
*Before you go to school this morning, please feed the dog.*
*Thanks,*
*Dad*

Seeing the note reminded the man and he inquired of his son, who was standing nearby.

"Did you feed the dog?" he asked, pointing to the note.

"No," replied the son. "I didn't see the note."

And it came to pass that when the father heard the answer of his son, he lost something; something very important.

Perhaps he wasn't paying attention.

Perhaps he had a mental lapse.

Maybe he was just too tired. For whatever reason, the man lost something he hadn't lost in a long, long time. He lost his temper. He became angry. He raised his voice, pointed his finger and severely rebuked his son for disobedience.

"I *know* you saw that note taped to the cabinet door!" shouted the man, in a loud, angry voice. "You deliberately chose to ignore me, and I don't appreciate being ignored!"

He scolded his son with sharp, combative words; he railed, bullied, and verbally abused his son. He accused the son of dishonesty, and the intensity of his stormy rage blew like a furious gale.

The man's son looked surprised, sorrowed, and sombered at the tongue-lashing he received. He was not accustomed to such loud talk and accusatory language from his good and decent father. He looked down at the floor as the father continued his barrage of words, biting words that broke his spirit.

The son did not respond. He did not defend. He just stood; head bowed, heart beating, hurt beyond words, hurt beneath tears.

Quiet returned to the kitchen after several moments. Sanity was restored. The father calmed down. He chatted with other family members about their day. He casually looked through the mail on the desk in the family room. He smiled as he scratched the ears of the family dog and went about the normal activities of a quiet evening at home with his loving family.

The man sat down in the overstuffed chair in the living room. He was fine now. He wanted to send a message to his family that he was fine. He didn't need their help finding his lost temper, as he needed their help finding his lost keys, or pocketknife, or pen. Control had been re-established.

*We'll just pretend the last several minutes didn't happen, and enjoy a quiet evening at home,* thought the man, as he leaned back in the overstuffed chair in the living room.

And the man forgot about losing his temper.

But the next morning, as the man sat in a boring administrative meeting, his memory left the conference room and he walked with his mind's eye back into his kitchen the previous evening. He stood, again, by the white pantry door and read the note he had left for his son.

And he remembered where he lost his temper.

---

♦

## As the two sat together talking and listening, acceptance sat down between them. Understanding pulled up a chair.

♦

---

He remembered his words, spoken in anger and rebuke. He saw the face of his son. He watched again the pain and confusion that brought a change to his son's countenance like the iris on the lens of a camera. The intensity of each glaring word caused the aperture of the boy's life to narrow and darken. The young man's face changed from open and honest to closed and fixed and dusk.

And as the man remembered that scene, he felt ashamed.

He walked briskly out the door of the conference room as soon as his meeting was finished. He drove to his son's high school campus. He scribbled "Appointment" on the parental sign-out sheet in the school office. Then, he stood and waited outside the office door until his son walked by, on his way to fourth period class.

"Simeon," said the father, "how about lunch?"

The son looked surprised to see his father at school, surprised and glad.

"Yeah, sure Dad," he said.

Soon, they sat in the quiet of a nearby restaurant and talked about their respective days of boredom—the father's in a meeting, and the son's in algebra. But before many moments had passed, their conversation turned to losings and findings.

"I ... uh ... I was wrong in what I said last night," said the father. He stumbled over words. Ineloquence made it difficult for his lips, but he continued to struggle until he had delivered his apology. "I'm ashamed that I lost my temper over something that wasn't even important. I've asked the Lord to forgive me, Sim. I need you to forgive me, too."

As the two sat together talking and listening, acceptance sat down between them.

Understanding pulled up a chair.

Repentance brought reconciliation to lunch, and the good and decent father found forgiveness in the eyes of his son.

> *Reckless words pierce like a sword,*
> *but the tongue of the wise brings healing.*
> (Prov. 12:18 NIV)

# ·2·

# It

Today is the day after Christmas. There's not much happening, so I'd like to show you around my office. Like many pastor's offices, mine is peppered with memorabilia and artifacts—things that have been given to me by family and friends. They serve as reminders of people I love and of fond experiences in my life.

If you were here, I'd show you pictures of my kids when they were still young and growing up. I have pictures of all three of them at various stages of their development. I'd show you Simeon's picture, the one I took when he was about three, wearing his "I was custom-made in Heaven" t-shirt. I'd show you the picture of Marcus the artist, sitting at a desk with two pencils, working on a masterpiece. You'd see a photo of Nate holding a fishing rod, wearing that old, red felt hat and his green jacket. Those pictures are special to me.

I save love notes from my wife Randee, too. Some of them are in my desk drawer, some on my shelves, so that when I'm having a particularly *interesting* day (I like to use the word *interesting* instead of *rotten*), I can walk over and read one of her notes. Great therapy for *interesting* days.

I have a wooden map of Belize, Central America, that my best friend, a missionary, gave me. There are candles I never light (my wife thought they would look good in my office) and a few things mounted on boards, like my degree and my certificate of ordination.

My shelves hold lots of books on all kinds of subjects, a couple of stuffed animals my wife gave me, and Grandpa's old watch encased in glass to protect it from dust. A couple of plastic plants (I kill the other kind) add color. A little cardboard placard sits on my bookshelf. It reads: *Any guy with hair on his head is over-dressed as far as I'm concerned.* Everything in my office, or almost everything, was given to me by a person I love and want to remember. Especially **IT**.

**IT** sits high and well-protected on the second shelf of my tallest bookcase, next to one of my Bibles. Two hand-carved wooden letters—**IT**—alone, stoic, and stolid as a two-inch wooden Indian. **IT** was a gift from my good friend, Lisa.

I had only been in my present pastorate for a few days when I met Lisa. She was a regular part of our weekly ministry to single adults. She loved music and brought her guitar to share songs she had written. Hers was a sad story, but Christ had restored her life, and she relished her walk with Him.

She was a good parent to two beautiful, bright daughters. She had many friends, and of course, there was Jesus. He was the theme of her song, the anchor that secured her life. She'd been through a lot and knew from experience that any other way was meaningless.

Within weeks of our first meeting, I noticed Lisa limping a bit. She thought she had twisted her knee, and we laughed about getting old.

She was 27.

Doctors eventually told Lisa she had a mysterious degenerative nerve disease that was very difficult to treat. Over the next few years, I watched Lisa go from walking on two legs to being confined to a wheelchair. She was in constant, excruciating pain. As her pastor and friend, I watched her frustration and listened to her story.

IT was one word that always came up.

IT made her mad. IT wasn't fair. IT was scary, lonely, and very difficult. At times, she would call me and say she thought she was "losing IT." After awhile, she said IT didn't matter anymore. Yet the longer I worked with Lisa, the more certain I was that IT did matter.

Frustrated doctors tried to relieve her pain. They eventually implanted an electronic device deep into Lisa's brain which they hoped would scramble the signal of pain from her legs.

My wife and I went to see her in the hospital the night before the surgery. They had shaved her head. Lisa told us the surgery was dangerous, and could leave her without the ability to speak, or sing, or even move. Some paralysis was almost certain.

We prayed.

We said good-bye, and the next day, Lisa went in to face **IT**. When she came out of surgery, she had lost the use of her right arm.

After a lengthy convalescence, doctors moved Lisa to a rehabilitation hospital for therapy: long hours of anguish interspersed with brief moments of total boredom. We talked during our visits about feelings and failures and the future. But **IT** came up most often.

**IT** hurt.

**IT** seemed like she had been in the hospital forever.

**IT** made her daughters cry when they had to leave their mother and stay with friends because Lisa was in the hospital for months.

For my fortieth birthday, a group of my friends got together to congratulate me on my passing "the half-way point." Several folks roasted me on the pitfalls of being forty. Before the evening was finished, Lisa made her way to the front, and presented me with one of my most cherished mementos: **IT**. Two letters, painfully carved by Lisa in beautiful wood as part of her physical therapy.

Lisa's condition continued to worsen, and she eventually had to give up caring for her children. **IT** made her feel guilty. She was virtually house-bound, and although she had many visitors, **IT** made her feel lonely. She tried to write, listen to tapes, and read. But **IT** became increasingly difficult. She would ask God why and wonder if today would be the day He would give her an answer. **IT** never came.

Friends brought Lisa to our candlelight communion service on Christmas Eve. She sat in her wheelchair, hands folded. I walked up to her and knelt to greet her. Pain said hello as she looked into my eyes.

"I had to come," she said. "I couldn't miss Christmas Eve."

A kind friend stopped by to see Lisa the next day and take her sick cat to the vet. She found Lisa lying in her bed asleep. But she was not asleep. She had *gone home.*

That was two years ago.

Real life isn't like a television program. In real life, innocent people suffer incredible things, and the things they suffer aren't wrapped in neat packages that get resolved by the end of the show. In real life, there are days when IT seems to be a long, long word, with complex meanings and implications. In life, there may be weeks and months and, yes, even years of enduring IT without a clue as to why IT has happened. Things such as:

- Why did my child's marriage fail?
- Why did my spouse have a nervous breakdown?
- Why does my child have this mental or physical handicap?
- Why did my baby die?

As difficult as those questions are, there are others even more debilitating and insidious. Was IT my fault? Was IT something I did? Could I have prevented IT?

So much of life is pockmarked with questions without answers. And I certainly don't have the inside track on life's deepest mysteries. But if you were here today, I'd show you a reminder Lisa left me—IT—a two-inch monument of faith sitting on the second shelf of my tallest bookcase.

IT may come to pass, and IT may be difficult, awful and filled with pain. But Christ has not forgotten.

The Man of Sorrows promised never to leave us, never to forsake us.

The One acquainted with grief has sent a Comforter, the Holy Spirit, to encourage us. And as if that were not enough, He left us three last words. Thank God, He left three triumphant words that we must never forget, the last words uttered this side of the tomb. One final blast in the face of life . . . and death . . . and IT:

*"It is finished!"*
(John 19:30)

# ◆3◆

# The Swimming Pool

**I**'ve always admired a man who knows what he wants, and then sets out to get it. Maybe that's one of the reasons I like Jerry Opperman so much. He and his family have been a part of our church for a long time. He looks like Oliver "Daddy" Warbucks in *Little Orphan Annie*. He has a row of short, gray-white hair around the back of his head, and its bald top shines like a brass doorknob in the morning sun. He's got four kids and one wife. But he *didn't* have a swimming pool . . . and he wanted one. So, he built one. But he didn't build it like everybody else.

I've known other people who wanted swimming pools built in their backyards. The process you follow is not complicated.

Call a swimming pool contractor.

Sit down with him and talk about budget, size, and shape of the pool.

Have him look at your backyard.

Talk about the schedule. When to begin. When to end.

Discuss how much it will cost. Lots of measuring and sketching on paper.

After the contractor has gathered all the necessary information, he goes back to his office and draws up the plans. When he comes back the next time, he brings a roll of blueprints with him . . . and his crew. They take down the fencing in the backyard. They bring in some equipment and trucks to haul away the dirt. They dig. They haul. They make a huge hole in the earth. They "rough-in" the plumbing and the filtering system. Then they line the sides of the hole with forms for concrete. They pour the walls and floor of the pool. They take their time, because they want to do a good job. And finally, they fill the pool with water. That's the way you build a pool.

Well, . . . that may be the way *you* would build a pool, but it certainly is not the way Jerry Opperman built his pool.

You see, Jerry is an iron worker by profession. He's been doing construction work for a long time. And when he thought about how much money it would cost to use someone else's design for his pool—how expensive it would be to have someone come out and build it—he couldn't see spending all that money just to have someone dig a hole, pour a little concrete around the edges, and fill it up with water.

So . . . he designed his own pool. He sat down at his kitchen table and drew a picture of what he thought he would like. He'd never done it before, but it didn't look that difficult. His wife Kathy helped with formulating the dream-pool. They decided on an odd-shaped pool, non-symmetrical; one-of-a-kind, I suppose you could say. They planned. They measured. They walked off the measurements in the backyard and drove stakes in the ground to outline their pool.

After several more weeks of planning and preparation, there was only one thing left to do. Begin.

One afternoon when Jerry got home from work, he went to his garage. He got his shovel and the old rusty wheelbarrow he'd had since he was a kid. He pushed that wheelbarrow around to the backyard.

Then, he spat on his hands, rubbed them together, and he started to dig. He filled the wheelbarrow with dirt, pushed it over to his property's edge, and dumped it. Just as he thought. Nothin' to it. He went back for another load. Three or four times he went back. Then he put the old wheelbarrow away, went into the house, and relaxed for the rest of the evening. The next night when he got home from work, he did the same thing. Filled and emptied the wheelbarrow four or five times . . . and then quit. Day in and day out. A lot of dirt. Over eight-hundred cubic yards of dirt he shoveled. He dug a hole forty-feet long, seventeen-feet wide at one end, and twenty-two feet wide at the other end—the deep end—the *very deep* end. Fifteen-feet down he dug at the deep end.

Day after day, week after week he poured work into his pool, a cupful at a time. His wife helped. His kids helped, too. Everyone in the family got to be a part of the great adventure of building the pool.

At the end of that year, the city tax assessor checked the construction permits issued during the preceding twelve months and noticed Jerry's pool permit. Houses are more expensive when they have pools. The more expensive they are, the higher the taxes on the house.

So, the tax assessor knocked on Jerry's door one day and said, "I'd like to see how you're coming along with your pool." He quickly saw that it wasn't finished, and said he'd be back "next year." The next year he did come back. Still not done.

He came back the year after that, and the year after that, and the year after that. In fact, for five years in a row he came to see Jerry's slowly developing pool, and each time it wasn't finished.

Finally, a few years ago, he told Jerry he thought he'd be better off just filling in the hole and calling it quits on the idea of building his own pool.

"Not on your life," was Jerry's response.

"Well, just give me a call if you ever get it done," scoffed the tax assessor, "and we'll figure the taxes then."

Some people don't have much faith, I guess. Just because Jerry's been working on his pool for such a long time, they think he'll never get finished. Well, it has been a while—a long while. Jerry's been working on that hole-in-the-ground for fourteen years. He's got fourteen years worth of stories about that bottomless pit. A lot of memories, and a lot of struggles. If you asked him, Jerry will tell you about the time the dirt caved in after a rain, and he had to shovel dirt for weeks just to get back to where he was before it all fell in. He'll show you pictures of the reinforcements he built to keep cave-ins from happening. Incredible. I've stood on the side of that cavernous hole myself, and I still can't believe one man moved all that dirt—with a wheelbarrow and shovel.

Next month we have a water baptism scheduled at Jerry's house. Just a few weeks ago, a swimming pool that took fourteen years to build was finally finished. A pool—a hand-dug, personally designed, poured-in-concrete swimming pool—was filled with water. Formidable. Deep. Significant.

Jerry has already invited us. Next month he wants to have the congregation over for a pool dedication and baptismal service—all in one big splash; sort of a culmination of Jerry's construction project and a celebration marking the beginning of new lives under construction by The Carpenter. I already know what I'm going to say. If I get to baptize any of those new converts, I'm going to remind them that Jesus drew up the plans for their lives Himself; detailed, challenging plans that will slowly take shape with the passing of every new day.

I'm going to tell them not to get too taxed if some things don't seem to be progressing as quickly as they would like. Wait and see. God's very patient, and He'll finish what He starts.

But there's no need to try to hurry Him along. He operates on His own eternal schedule, and I've been noticing lately that He seems to enjoy the process of building deep and abiding things . . . a little at a time.

> *. . . He who has begun a good work in you*
> *will complete it until*
> *the day of Jesus Christ.*
> (Phil. 1:6)

# ·4·

# When You're All Out of Noodles

I'm not a cook.

I can fry an edible egg, and have been known to fix a mouth-watering bologna sandwich now and then, but I could hardly be considered a cook. I am a *reader*. When I cook, I *read* cookbooks.

When my children were much younger, I would occasionally stay home from my office and play Mr. Mom while Randee taught kindergarten. On one particular occasion, after I had driven my wife to school, I decided to prepare dinner for the family. It was early morning, so I had plenty of time for planning and preparation.

When I arrived back home, I looked for the fattest cookbook I could find and began reading. (I looked for a big cookbook because I need the extra stimulus of *pictures* of the food when I cook, and most big cookbooks have pictures.) Soon I found it—beef Stroganoff. The picture looked absolutely delicious, so that's what I chose. It seemed to me that there were no mysterious ingredients in the recipe: stew meat, various herbs and seasonings, sour cream . . . and noodles.

*No big deal, I thought. I'll put the meat and seasonings into the slow-cooker, turn that baby on, and within a few hours, I'll have something to pour over the noodles.*

There was a certain smugness in my walk to the freezer to get the stew meat for the Stroganoff. Randee would be so pleased and surprised. It would be so easy, too. I'd be a hero without breaking a sweat.

Within minutes, the slow-cooker was half-filled with meat. I turned it on high, put on the glass cover, and shoved it into its corner of the counter. I gave the red-checkered cookbook sitting nearby a quick, final glance.

*Oh, yeah. Noodles. I'd better check and make sure we've got some noodles,* I thought. The sound of cabinet doors opening and closing filled our house for the next several minutes. I looked in every cupboard and cubbyhole. I even asked five-year-old Nathan if he knew where Mommy keeps her noodles?

"No, Daddy. I don't think she has no noodles."

I don't know if the frustration of *not* having what you need when you're cooking is common to all cooks. But it is common to *this* cook. I became emotional over not having any noodles in the house. And, as is often the case when I am emotional, I made a decision *based* on emotion. I decided that if we didn't *have* any noodles, I would just *make* some noodles. Back to my red-checkered cookbook.

I looked up "noodles." In addition to a great recipe and ingredient list, I found a series of pictures of a lady in an apron which carefully documented the process for making homemade noodles.

*Doesn't look as though they're that hard to make,* I thought.

I donned one of my wife's aprons—after all, the lady in the picture was wearing one—and propped up the cookbook so I could read the directions easily and see the pictures of how to do it. I got the biggest bowl I could find and began.

First, I gathered up all the necessary ingredients: a little flour, a little shortening, a couple of eggs, and some milk. I already knew where most everything was, because I'd looked in every cabinet in the house for the noodles! Within minutes, I'd have some wonderful noodles. She'd be so glad when she got home.

I had watched my wife "double" recipes on occasion when she wanted to have plenty of whatever she was cooking. I wanted to make lots of noodles, . . . so I went for it. I put twice the ingredients called for into my big bowl, and mixed them, like the lady in the picture.

*Looks kinda dry,* I thought. *Trying to mix these ingredients would be easier if there were more moisture in the bowl.* I resisted the temptation to add more milk or water to the flour, however, and continued to stir and mix the dough. I mixed until *it* was a ball and *I* was a mess. I noticed as I mixed and messed with the dough that there seemed to be a correlation between how gooey my hands were and how itchy my nose got. I suppressed my urge to scratch it, however, and instead looked back at the cookbook to see how I was doing.

The directions in the book confirmed the obvious. The dough *was* definitely a ball. In fact, it was about the size of a bowling ball. When I took my dough out of the bowl, I held it next to the picture in the book. Mine looked quite a bit larger, but undaunted, I proceeded to the next step:

**Directions:**
    On a large baking board, roll the dough until it is paper-thin and translucent. *(Sprinkle the board and the dough with extra flour to minimize sticking.)*

I am a literalist. If the Bible says God created everything in six days, well, then . . . And if the red-checkered cookbook says one-quarter cup, I add one-quarter cup—exactly—no more, and no less. And if the cookbook says "paper-thin and translucent," that must mean thin as a newspaper. Roll that dough until it's ultra-thin and you can see light passing through it.

I took the rolling pin, and with my elbows out, and all my weight bearing down on the bowling-ball-shaped dough, I rolled. Within seconds, I determined that I did indeed have a "sticking" problem with my dough. It stuck everywhere. It stuck to the rolling pin. It stuck to the baking board. When I tried to "unstick" it, it stuck to my fingers.

The baking directions failed to give complete instructions on how to get extra flour out of the bag if both your hands are totally covered—all ten fingers—with gooey dough. I used my imagination (and my elbows) to turn the bag of flour that was sitting on the counter top out onto the baking board. The book was right, however; extra flour reduces sticking, and soon I was rolling the dough out on the board.

As you might imagine, the longer I rolled the dough, the wider it spread, and the more space it required. It fanned out over the edge of the counter. In fact, it drooped down the countertop—about the size of a full page of newsprint and growing with every pass of the rolling pin. I had visions of a sheet of dough the size of a twin bed before I was through.

I finally picked up my dough, and held it up to the light. *Translucent all right,* I thought to myself. I laid the dough aside, now, and checked the directions again. What I read seemed logical.

**Directions:**
Hang the dough in a cool, dry place for one to two hours to dry before rolling it into a roll and slicing it into one-half-inch strips.

There was no picture in the book of "a cool, dry place." I assumed at that point that the cook was left to his own devices, and I began searching for a suitable spot to hang my dough.

The wrought iron banister would be perfect. It separated the dining room from the living room. It was cool. It was dry. It was long (for my dough needed a lot of room) and it was available. I took a bucket of warm, soapy water, and I scrubbed the banister from top to bottom. Then, almost ceremoniously, I hung my dough over that banister like a mother hangs a baby blanket over a line to dry.

"What you doin' Dad?" Nathan asked. I didn't even *try* to explain.

About an hour and a half. That's how long that noodle-dough hung on the banister. I'm sure it was an hour and a half, because that's how long it took me to clean up the mess in the kitchen. Flour was everywhere. It was in my hair. It was in my eyes. I'm still trying to figure out how I got that sticky dough in my back pocket.

Every measuring cup and spoon in the entire house was dirty, (along with most of the dishes). The flour on the kitchen floor started just east of the door and ran like wagon tracks west into the rest of the house. Determination helped me get it all cleaned up—no flour on the floor, no dough on the banister. Everything was tidy and neat.

When my wife came home that night, two well-scrubbed children and one loving husband—and the smell of beef Stroganoff—greeted her at the door. She seemed pleased that I had cooked something, but when she noticed *what* I had cooked for dinner, she confessed, "We'll have to go buy some noodles for your Stroganoff. I'm all out of noodles." That's when she saw them.

She walked by the green bowl—the large, wide, green bowl with the noodles in it. I had covered the noodles with a damp cloth (as the book said to do.) She pulled the cloth back and saw the noodles. I will *never* forget her response.

*Randee:* Where'd the noodles come from?
*Me:* I made them.
*Randee:* You did not. *Those* noodles are better than my *mother* can make!
*Me:* I don't know about that. I just know I made those noodles.

She bragged on me. She hugged my neck. She told me she couldn't believe I did it. She ran her fingers through those noodles, and marveled at how perfect they were, how evenly they were cut ... paper-thin and translucent. She looked at me with misty eyes and said I was incredible.

There have been other times, of course, when my wife has looked at me with misty eyes, times when I haven't been as sensitive as I should, times when a careless word or attitude caused pain; times when I've looked back on my own actions and thought to myself, *How could I be so dumb!*

I try to avoid those times, because I really do want to be a good husband. But finding the right ingredients is a difficult challenge. God has always known that, of course. That's why He wrote down the directions.

God wrote down the directions for how to be a loving, caring husband. The best part of the directions was the personal demonstration He gave us. The Bridegroom painted a sacrificial picture for the whole world of what it meant to be vulnerable and open. He left His celestial surroundings to walk among us—paper-thin and translucent—so we could see the Light.

Then, He hung in the wind, dry and parched, to die—a fantastic picture of what it means to serve; an Eternal Portrait of what it's like to give and care and love.

*Husbands, love your wives,*
*just as Christ also loved the church*
*and gave Himself for her.*
(Eph. 5:25)

# .5.

# Ambient Noise

On many mornings I drive to a small, out-of-the-way coffeehouse near my home, hoping to spend a few moments of quiet reflection and to write in my journal. I have a certain seat I like, right next to a window where the light is good for reading. I get there early, just after they open, to assure that I can have my spot.

I order coffee, take my Bible and journal from my satchel, and I read . . . and write . . . and think. I enjoy the quiet; not too many customers are there that early in the morning; soft classical music is in the background. I look forward to the routine of such solitude . . . but yesterday was *not* routine.

For yesterday, as I got out of my car and walked up to the coffeehouse, I noticed workmen wearing white overalls and paint-splattered hats. They stood next to a truck parked in front of the coffeehouse. Even though it was barely light, I could see that they readied buckets and brushes and tarpaulins. *Painters*, I thought. *Must be gonna paint something today.*

I gave the workers a friendly nod as I walked by them and into the door of the coffeehouse and proceeded with my ritual. I ordered my coffee. I took my seat in the corner next to the window. And I settled back in quiet reflection upon the deeper things of life. But as I started to read my Bible and write in my journal, *they* started too . . . or maybe I should say *it* started too . . . the noise, I mean.

As soft classical music played bravely in the background, a most annoying barrage of barbarous sound began: a scraping noise, a noise so obnoxious that it rivaled a dentist's drill or fingernails sliding down a blackboard.

Right outside the window next to *my* chair, a painter started scraping the old paint off *my* windowsill. He assaulted the sill and the side of the building with loud, long drags of a paint scraper. I watched as he began to joke and laugh, screeching and scratching all over my solitude.

I didn't last long in the coffee house yesterday morning. Within a few minutes of sitting down, I had to leave. My entire day lagged and limped along because my morning routine had been disrupted.

I knew better than to try to go back to the coffeehouse this morning. I'm sure they're still at it. It takes more than one day to paint an entire building: more scraping and laughing; more distractions and disturbing noise. So this morning, I just drove to my office at the appointed time and forgot about the coffee and the reading and the writing in my journal. I need quiet for such things.

As I walked through the door to our offices, however, I noticed something I had never seen before, something new on the floor immediately outside our Christian counseling center office. It was round, about the size of a dessert plate, and plugged into the wall, giving out a constant noise. It wasn't a loud noise, just constant. I'd describe it as a poor imitation of the wind blowing through pine needles and aspen leaves, or maybe a feeble attempt at the sound of waves constantly washing up on the beach—a quiet, constant noise. *What in the world is that thing?* I thought to myself as I stopped in the hall to stare. I had several guesses, but few clues.

I finally asked the receptionist about it. She said, "It's an ambient noise generator. If it's too quiet in here, we can distinguish the voices in the counseling offices and we want to protect their privacy. So we got the noise generator to cover the voices." Her explanation made perfect sense to me, but didn't it have to be louder to mask the conversations, I asked. "No," she said. "The constancy of the sound tricks the ear so that what is being said can't be distinguished."

*Interesting*, I thought. *Very interesting*. One kind of noise to cover the sound of another.

♦

No wonder, Lord. No wonder I strain to hear what You have to say to me. As life's frustrations and interruptions scrape by the window of my life, the volume and the texture and the timbre of the noise so annoy me that I am distracted, an all-too-easy victim of a life-learning disability.

I'm convinced I have a spiritual attention deficit disorder.

The disappointing thing is that it need not be a loud, raucous noise to confound me. The constancy of sound—little noises, soft, inward, ambient thoughts and fears and attitudes—tricks the ears of my inner man and masks Your still, small voice.

Help me today, Lord, to find that listening-post, that quiet place, that place of Light, where I can escape the confounding and confusing noise . . . and linger in the presence of Your holiness.

> . . . *the effect of righteousness [will be]*
> *quietness.*
> (Isa. 32:17)

# ·6·

# Known Only to God

Sometimes when I tell stories, people ask me if they are true. And I say to them, "Yes, they are true stories, and yes, they really did happen." Usually, the one who has asked the question will smile and nod, and I will smile and nod back.

It's always nice to write a story that brings warmth and encouragement to another. But sometimes, . . . sometimes, stories must be told that are not warm and encouraging. Sometimes, stories must be told that are tragic and awful. The words used for such stories are hard words, sharp words that paint black pictures. I will tell you this story without compromise or apology . . . because I am sad.

♦

The line at the cleaners seemed stalled as my wife and

I waited our turn. My wife noticed the mother of a former student of hers come in with an armful of clothes. They smiled and greeted one another, and while I held our place in line, my wife walked to the back and talked with the woman. "And how is Nancy?" I heard my wife ask. Nancy (not her real name) had been her student a few years before, in the seventh grade.

"Oh, she's okay now, I guess. The last three months have been difficult, though." The mother fidgeted with the weight of the clothes in her arms, as she lowered her voice and motioned Randee to come closer. "We found out that Nancy was . . . you know," her voice dropped to a whisper, . . . . "pregnant." The woman leaned in toward my wife, and I watched as the two now talked quietly.

When you've been married for a long time, you learn to read the face of your mate. You don't read her face like you read a newspaper in the morning while you drink your coffee. It's a different kind of reading; not words, but reading just the same.

And as I stood in line at the cleaners, I read my wife's face, and I knew she was listening to a sad story. Randee's facial expressions changed as the conversation continued in the cleaners that day. When we got in the car, she told me the story she had heard.

Nancy had been a troubled child from the beginning, it seemed. Even in Randee's seventh grade class, she was rebellious and difficult. But Randee enjoyed teaching her, and Nancy seemed to make some progress, both academically and behaviorally. Her mother said that when she entered ninth grade, she became much more difficult to handle. Nancy became sexually active in the ninth grade. Her parents warned her, and scolded her. They tried grounding her and restricting her freedom. Nothing seemed to work.

Nancy was determined. She had run away twice in the last two-and-a-half years. Both times when she came back home, she told her parents she was old enough to make her own decisions.

She was old enough to have a baby, too. And three months ago, she sat down at the kitchen table with her mom and dad and told them she was pregnant. The parents feared all along that such a thing would happen. But Nancy assured them that she was responsible about her life-style and would take "precautions" to avoid such "complications" as pregnancy.

But Nancy was not responsible. She was promiscuous, and rebellious and seventeen and . . . pregnant.

Nancy's parents knew there were alternatives to a seventeen-year-old giving birth. They knew that if they didn't want *their* baby to give birth to a baby, there was a choice in the matter. So, they took her to a clinic, and sat and talked to a "counselor" about options. They signed some papers, made an appointment, and said they'd be back in a few days.

Last Tuesday morning, Nancy's parents drove her across town to that same clinic, an abortion clinic. They watched as Nancy was greeted by a friendly receptionist who took her into the back of the clinic. And as that mother and father sat in a waiting room sipping black coffee, reading old copies of *Readers Digest*, not thirty feet away behind a closed door in another room, their daughter—their baby—climbed up on a table, spread her seventeen-year-old legs and allowed a masked doctor to suck a baby out of her womb. When the procedure was completed, the doctor came out to talk with the parents.

"Everything went well. Nancy's doing just fine. We'll leave her in the recovery area for a little while, and then you can take her home," said the young doctor with the mask now pulled below his chin. The mother expressed concern for her daughter and choked back emotion at the thought of aborting her first grandchild.

The doctor knew just what to say. With a pat on her hand, he assured her they had made the right decision. "The fetus was deformed, and if the pregnancy had been allowed to go full-term, the baby would have been born with serious problems. It's better this way," said the doctor, as he stood and prepared to raise his mask for another appointment, with another pregnant woman . . . and another baby.

I am sad today because there is much pain in this story: the pain of a seventeen-year-old rebellious child whose choices resulted in an unwanted pregnancy; the pain of tearful parents who watched their daughter making those bad choices, and then were faced with difficult choices of their own. My heart is heavy for that daughter and that mom and that dad. I grieve for them. I do.

But most of all, I cry for that baby. I do not weep for "the product of conception." I weep for that child—that first grandchild—the "deformed one" that a nameless, faceless doctor said had no right to be born—and no choice but to die.

I cry for the baby whose name is known only to God—the baby who was made in the image of God—the one they left in a bucket in the back of that clinic. I know. Babies die every day, and that is sad. Thousands of nameless babies are aborted every day, and that is tragic. But I don't know those babies. I do know one baby, who died last week, last Tuesday . . . and I cry because I am sad.

*For a voice of wailing is heard . . . "How we are plundered!*
*We are greatly ashamed . . ."*
*For death has come through our windows,*
*Has entered our palaces,*
*To kill off the children—no longer to be outside!*
*And the young men—no longer on the streets!*
(Jer. 9:19, 21)

## ·7·

# Original Joe's

When the Lord God was thinking about how to knit a man together, He took the yarn of recollection and created a memory. He made remembering part of the fabric of every human being. He sewed recall into the garment of every person—a common fiber, yet unique to every man and woman; a Divine design to keep things in perspective ... and He stood back and said, "This is good."

Later, when the Lord God wanted to write a Book for man on how to live a good and happy life, He wondered how He should begin. He finally settled upon four carefully chosen words; four words that men could use as a reference beacon when the way became difficult to see: "In the beginning, God ..."

◆

Last week was a particularly difficult one for my wife

and me, so on Friday we took a drive. Pressing matters had mashed us up against the walls of life. Uncertainty about the future made us nervous. A variety of "stuff" had crowded our lives into a corner, like too many people on an elevator. Our personal space was being violated, and we found ourselves pushing and shoving—not against each other, but against *life*. We'd had enough. *Time to take a break and get away from the crowd*, we thought—a mini-vacation for a day.

So, on Friday, we took off. We left a note stuck on the front door for our three sons who were out running errands when we left. We were going on a date. We didn't know exactly where, but we'd call and leave a message to let them know. We wouldn't be back until late.

We drove thirty-five miles south of our home to one of those home shows. You know the kind I mean: booths set up in a large convention center where businesses show off the latest in trash compactors and refrigerators and stoves; "how-to" demonstrations on everything from furniture strippers to vegetable mutilators (they call them slicers); videos on stuff like how to build a redwood deck that will stand up to the weather. It was all there.

We held hands and strolled along, not saying much. We didn't hurry. We didn't look at our watches. We didn't *care*. We just held hands and walked around that huge convention center looking at the displays and listening to the sales pitches tossed our way by the various vendors. It felt good to have no agenda. About five o'clock, we got hungry and decided to eat. Original Joe's was only a block away.

Original Joe's is a restaurant. It has no panoramic view; only a marginal atmosphere and reasonable prices for good food, but nothing particularly noteworthy to even be included in this book, except—except for the fact that Original Joe's was the first place I ever took my wife on a date. Before we were married, before there was a ministry or children or the challenges of life together . . . our first date was to have dinner at Original Joe's. The place is still there, and last week, we went back.

While we waited for our dinner to be served, we talked. We sipped ice water, talked about money, the household budget, and kids going to college. We wrestled with the *stuff* of life . . . stuff like our two cars. Neither of them exactly "run"; they sort of *mope*. We needed to decide what to do about our growing transportation problems . . . so we talked. We talked about our home, too. It's altogether possible our "nest" will be empty soon. What of the future? How are we doing with our long-range goals? Randee dreams of one day developing an educational consulting service for the parents of kids with learning disabilities. But she doesn't know how to begin. So on Friday, as we sat waiting at Original Joe's , we talked about how that might happen. We grappled with other difficult issues, too—personal issues not meant for telling in books, not meant for saying out loud so someone sitting in the next booth could hear. We took turns talking softly and listening carefully; listening to each other's fears and dreams and . . . hearts.

The nice part of a day like last Friday, though, was not all the talk we did about the vicissitudes of life. It was the romance of remembering. Before our conversation was finished, we spent some time remembering the way it was the first time . . . the first time we ever went to Original Joe's. I pointed out the booth where we sat; Randee had forgotten. She did remember what she ordered: steak with mushrooms. We chatted about other stuff, too, quiet stuff, romantic, boy-girl stuff.

It wasn't an earth-shattering thing that happened last Friday, but it was significant, in that it provided an opportunity to get *life* back into perspective. If you're like me, sometimes it seems as if you're standing in an elevator, and too many people have gotten on. There's no more room for anything or anyone else and your comfort zone is being threatened. Each day becomes not a *slice* of life, but a mutilated mishmash that's difficult to handle. If that's where you are—if it's Thursday evening, and you don't think you can look another Friday in the face—maybe this story will help.

Leave a note on your door for all the people who think they need you. Tell them you'll be back, but you need some time—a day, maybe. Tell them you're going to look at trash compactors to see if you can come up with any ideas on what to do with some of the junk you're dealing with, to learn how to build a home that will weather the storms of life's winter rain.

And while you're at it, stop by your Original Joe's. Every marriage has one. If it's too far away to go there physically, then find another spot like it, and walk with your memory back to that place . . . the place where it all began.

> *In the beginning, God . . .*
> (Gen. 1:1)

# ·8·

# Idol Words

I've never been troubled with it before, but this morning as I sat at my desk reading, a bothersome thought crossed my mind. The more I dwelt on it, the more it nagged at me . . . something I think I forgot. I'm not sure there's much I can do about it now. Maybe that's the reason I was troubled. It has to do with teaching my children to talk.

You see, about twenty years ago, when Marcus, my oldest son, was nearly two, my wife and I began to teach him to talk. He kept it up, and now he can talk pretty well. In fact, he's a communications major in college. When Nathan was about two, we started teaching *him* to talk. He's still at it. And of course, we couldn't leave Simeon out. He's sixteen now, but about fourteen years or so ago, we began to coach him to talk. We tried to get him to mimic us. We pointed to objects like *birds* and *cars* and did our best to get him to say those words. We'd had plenty of experience by the time Simeon came along, so our teaching was easier.

We probably made fools of ourselves trying to get our kids to talk; after all, most people do. We'd laugh at their attempts at language and applaud when they even came *close* to identifying a household object correctly. I believe that the human voice is one of the most wonderful sounds God ever created. Every time one of our kids began to talk, it seemed that another note was added to the song of our home. We marveled at these infantile expressions formed in the depths of their own experiences and discoveries.

Teaching our kids to talk brought tremendous joy to Randee and me. We taught them to be careful about their language; that words can hurt; that some words are inappropriate. We taught them the little song, "Be careful, little mouths, what you say." We wanted them to know the power of the tongue and the harm it can bring if not harnessed.

But there's a problem I thought of this morning. When my wife and I taught our kids to talk, I don't ever recall telling them to be thrifty with their words. I don't ever remember mentioning that *words* need to be measured and carefully meted out. I don't know why I didn't say something about it then. Maybe I was too enamored with the sounds of their little voices. Maybe I was busy enjoying their talking. I don't know for certain why I never mentioned it, but the thought occurred to me this morning.

Talk is good. Talking must be good, because God could have created us all to be mutes if He hadn't liked the idea of speech. But too much talk—too many words that haven't been thought-out—have a deleterious effect on human beings.

I wish I'd have mentioned it to my kids along the way. I wish I'd have mentioned that men need to be careful not to make idol words out of idle words, to go on and on about nothing, and to become too familiar and fascinated with the sound of their own voices. The more infatuated we become with the sound of our own voices, the less likely we are to be interested in listening to someone else, someone else's story, and life.

As a pastor, in fact, I think I have a particular vulnerability to idol words. One pastor friend of mine told me that he had heard somewhere that if all the words a pastor preached in a given year were set end-to-end, they'd be the equivalent of six novels. Maybe that's why I was troubled this morning. I'm a pastor . . . and I'm a writer . . . and I agree with the rest of what my friend had to say: Ain't nobody writes six good books a year!

*My dear brothers, take note of this:*
*Everyone should be quick to listen,*
*slow to speak.*
(James 1:19 NIV)

# ·9·

# The Smells of Thanksgiving

I love Thanksgiving. I always have. I remember growing up that Thanksgiving day was different from any other day of the year. On most Thanksgivings, the air in our neighborhood hung heavy with the smell of roasting turkey coming from almost every house. But roasting turkey wasn't the only smell.

In our neighborhood, Thanksgiving day was sort of the last day to burn leaves before winter's snow started falling. Several of the dads in our neighborhood would come out of their homes early on that morning and rake leaves into piles and burn them. I loved the sound that Thanksgiving always made: the sound of rakes scratching at leaves; the sound of talk about life as men leaned on their rakes and watched the leaves burn. I loved the smell, too; the smell of burning leaves, mixed with Thanksgiving turkeys cooking in almost every house.

Like most people, I suppose, I have many wonderful memories about times of gathering with family and friends. We usually had lots of relatives over for Thanksgiving. Our table on Thanksgiving always looked as if it had been transported from a church potluck dinner just before they said "Grace," totally covered with bowls of good things just begging to be eaten. For some reason, I was always hungrier on Thanksgiving than any other day of the year. Just the smell of a turkey cooking was almost enough to starve me to death—almost, but not quite.

I would check the progress of the dinner every few minutes, dipping and pinching and tasting my way into the kitchen. My mother seemed tolerant of my attempts to sneak premature bites of dressing or turkey—tolerant, but not oblivious. At regular intervals, she would shoo me out, with a reassuring "It'll be just a few more minutes, and then we can eat. I know you're starved." Well, as I said, I wasn't exactly starved, but I was plenty hungry . . . and it was hard to be patient. My memories of Thanksgiving dinners at home are treasured ones, but one particular celebration stands out from all the rest.

The relatives we usually shared our Thanksgiving with had made other plans, and we would be eating alone—just the five of us—my mom and dad and the three kids. When my mother finally called us to the table, we were ready. Even though we were starving, we knew from previous personal experience that wrestling for position like children in line at a water fountain could be hazardous. My folks were old-fashioned, I suppose, but they reacted rather strongly to children who ran to the table, pushing and shoving for a place to sit. So, our march to dinner was orderly and quiet . . . but with a great deal of anticipation.

We were all seated in our appointed places: my brother Dan and I sat next to each other; my little sister, who was about seven, sat on the end next to my mom. After Mom had taken her seat, we all looked to my dad, who prayed a special Thanksgiving prayer, thanking God for all He'd done and for the wonderful meal we were about to enjoy. But moments after the "Amen," there was a knock at the front door.

"Must be somebody wanting to play," said my brother Dan.

"Candy," said my mom, "will you go to the door and tell them we're just starting to eat. They'll have to come back later." My little sister obediently rose from the table and walked from the dining room through the house to tell the neighbor kid we couldn't play right now.

Within a few moments, she returned from her trip to the front door, took her seat at the end of the table and began filling her plate with savory things to eat. Dan wanted to know who was at the door. Was it Richard Justice, his buddy who lived across the street? Was it Mike Marler, who lived next door?

"No," said Candy. "I think he was a hobo."

Unison is a strange thing. Sometimes, when people hear things that they can't believe they've heard, they respond in an unrehearsed unison question of clarification; one or two words spoken by several people all at once, spoken as they lean toward the one who has just uttered the unbelievable. That's what we did.

My brother and I and my mom and dad all spoke in unison, "A hobo?"

Candy looked startled at our question. She stopped spooning candied yams onto her plate, stalled in mid-air as if she'd just been caught doing something wrong. "I think so," she said. "I *think* he was a hobo. He said he was hungry, and did we have anything to eat?"

My mother leaned toward my little sister as if the words were coming too slowly, as if she wanted Candy to get to the bottom line—the response. "What did you say, Candy? What did you tell him?" The urgency in my mother's voice made me know that something serious had just knocked on the door of our Thanksgiving.

"I told him we were just starting to eat, and he'd have to come back later. Isn't that what you *said* to say?" It was a correct answer that was clearly incorrect, an answer from someone too young to understand the irony of her words. Now, my mother sprang to her feet. Like a fireman answering a call, she raced to the front door, threw it open, and looked for the hungry stranger. He was not there. He had gone away. Across the lawn and out onto the sidewalk she ran, looking determined and urgent in her step. We all followed, a serpentine search party looking for the man who said he was hungry. We saw him walking, a few doors down from our house, his hands in his pockets, a brimmed hat on his bowed head, his eyes looking down as he walked.

She ran down the street, did my mother. She startled the man, I think, when she grabbed his arm. "Are you hungry? Are you the one who knocked on our door?" The man nodded, almost apologetically.

"Yes ma'am. I'm sorry to have disturbed your Thanksgiving," he said.

My mother did not seem disturbed. She seemed benevolent. She seemed resolute and understanding and . . . Christian about what to do when a hungry someone knocks on your door on Thanksgiving.

"Come with me," said my bold, four-foot-eleven-inch mother, as she guided the hungry man back to our house. My dad ushered him toward a seat in the living room and visited with the stranger as my mother disappeared into the kitchen. I listened to their conversation. My dad spoke to the man with dignity and genuine interest, ignoring his unkempt appearance. I do not remember the content of their conversation, only its warmth and concern. My mother soon reappeared from the dining room where she had set another place at our table.

"Please join us at the table," she invited. "You are welcome here, and we have more than enough food to share."

The hungry man ate with dirty hands, but he cleaned his plate. After he finished, he politely thanked my mother and said he needed to be moving on. She had prepared a sack lunch for him, and she and my dad walked him to the door and wished him well as he went on his way. I remember peeking out the front window as the stranger left. Even though I was just a little boy then, I have never forgotten watching him walk down the sidewalk and disappear into the anonymity of the city streets. And I've never forgotten the example of my parents on how to extend hospitality to someone who happens by.

My wife and I have had a parade of people go through our home during the course of our marriage; some of them came on Thanksgiving Day, and some of them came on ordinary days that we chose to fill with thanksgiving.

We carried some of those people up the steps in wheelchairs to get them into our house. We strained to understand some of them, because they spoke very little English.

Some were single moms with kids. Some were elderly people with no family. Orphans and refugees have graced our table. All of them have had one thing in common: They all needed love and understanding.

God's blessed most of us with more than we need. We don't have to wait for Thanksgiving to express our gratitude. Genuine thanksgiving needs to be celebrated every day by the people of God. Every day, lost people walk by the neighborhoods of our lives; people starving for answers, longing for rest. We need to leave the doors of our lives standing wide open. If the people walking by smell the Bread of Life, who knows?

Maybe they'll walk up to the Door, join the family of God, take a seat in the household of faith.

> *For we are to God the aroma of Christ*
> *among those who are being saved*
> *and those who are perishing.*
> (2 Cor. 2:15 NIV)

# ·10·

# Mrs. Berryman's Song

Sometimes when I wake up in the morning, a song will echo through my head. It might be a church song I haven't heard in years or a particular movement of a piece of classical music. I don't always hear music when I awake, but this morning I did.

Early this morning, I heard Mrs. Berryman singing, plain as day. Before the sun ever said "Good" to this morning, before any of the neighborhood dogs had stretched and yawned and barked, I heard Mrs. Berryman's song in my soul. She didn't write it. She just sang it to me one day, and it almost seemed as if I could hear her singing it again.

The Berrymans were members of the church where I served as associate pastor—one of my first *real* pastoral positions after graduating from college. But they were more than just members of the church. They also served on the church staff as custodians. They were retired, and every weekday, Monday through Friday, they cleaned the church. Their son, who was in his late twenties or early thirties and had physical and learning disabilities, came with them to help.

I noticed the Berrymans each morning, as they drove their old gray Chevy into the church parking lot. I could see them from my office window, and I would watch Mr. Berryman get out of the car. I could tell by the way he walked that the chill of Midwest winter mornings made it difficult to convince his arthritic back that it really was time to get moving. I watched him walk around the car to open the door for his wife. He didn't hurry, like a young man on a mission. Instead, he ambled, slowly with short, tired steps, like molasses dripping off a spoon: sweet . . . but slow.

I noticed the Berrymans' son, too, a simple young man, with uncomplicated motives. His job was to clean the church every day with his parents, and that's exactly what he did. Because his parents were elderly and had certain physical limitations, he managed most of the heavier tasks, like dumping trash, moving the heavy floor polisher around the multi-level building, and assisting in the interminable "set-up and take-down" of any large church campus. He seemed to really enjoy his work and to have a genuine love for God. Even though his learning problems made communicating with others more difficult, congregation members who would stop by the church offices during the week always enjoyed talking to him.

I loved to watch the Berrymans at work. "Clean" is a relative word for some people, but for the Berrymans it was an "absolute." If the church wasn't *absolutely clean* on Sunday mornings when all the congregation arrived, they took it personally. If the building and its grounds weren't in impeccable condition for the Wednesday night prayer meeting, with tile floors that gleamed from being buffed and polished and a nursery that was as sanitized as a hospital operating room, then they felt responsible.

So, when they cleaned the church, they *cleaned* it. I could hear them talk in the hall about the nursery, as I sat in my office on cold winter mornings, with many "Have you wiped-down all the cribs with disinfectant yet?" sorts of questions. While my young pastor mind tried to concentrate on a Bible class I was to teach on Sundays, they talked about the set-up for the room where the women's prayer meeting was held every Tuesday morning. The chairs had to be ready when the women arrived. The Berrymans wanted to make certain that the women who had come to pray wasted no time shuffling chairs.

Week after week, I could hear Mr. Berryman and his son struggle to push the heavy floor polisher down the hall. The whir of buffing brushes was a common background noise for my counseling appointments or study. In fact, on more than one occasion the distraction of the Berrymans trying to clean—vacuum and empty trash and dust—interrupted my study time and drove me to the quieter confines of my study at home.

But what of the song? The song I heard this morning?

Well, one ordinary Tuesday morning, I sat trying to study in my office. I knew *exactly* where Mrs. Berryman was. She was cleaning the men's rest room. I had seen her hand-scrawled sign taped to its door when I arrived:

> *I'm cleaning hear.*
> Mrs. Berryman

She had propped the door open with a large, gray plastic trash bin and cart, the one on wheels so she could push it easily, the one with the bottles of cleaning supplies and disinfectants and toilet brushes on it. I'd seen that cart many times, and I had read Mrs. Berryman's sign before, too. I knew exactly where Mrs. Berryman was.

The women of the church had gathered for their weekly prayer meeting for the missionaries. I listened to their distracting chatter as they came into the church and walked right by my office. I waited several seconds for the sound of their voices to finally fade away, and as they walked on down the hall—talking with each other on their way to talk with God—I was glad I could get back to my studies. I was very busy.

So was Mr. Berryman. He and his son had carried the floor buffer up the steps at the end of the hall, and I could hear its whine and dull roar through the ceiling of my office, which was right below them. *The noise isn't too loud,* I told myself, as I focused on my notes for my class the following Sunday. *More like a distant drone than a distraction,* I said to myself. *I don't know why they have to do this stuff now, while I'm trying to prepare for ministry, but I'll just ignore it and shut it out.* I shut the shutters of my mind to the busyness and distraction of the people all around me. I steeled myself to their inconsiderate noise and nerve—the nerve to clutter my study time with the noise of cleaning.

But as I sat in my office on that Tuesday morning, God would not ignore my ignorance. It was almost as if He said, "I'm cleaning. Hear! Listen up, so you won't miss the real sound of servanthood." In the midst of my pity party—in the midst of my pious study—school convened.

I heard something, and as I listened, I learned. I heard the voice of an old woman singing. The song was slightly muffled, but I could understand every word she sang, coming through the south wall of my office—the wall shared by the men's rest room. I could hear her voice, slow and sweet—sweet as molasses pouring from a spoon. And I could hear the toilet brush as it swished in the bowl. Mrs. Berryman was cleaning God's house. And as she cleaned, she sang this haunting song:

> I wonder, have I done my best for Jesus,
> > Who died upon the cruel tree?
> To think of His great sacrifice on Calv'ry,
> > I know my Lord expects the best from me.
> How many are the lost that I have lifted?
> > How many are the chained I've helped to free?
> I wonder, have I done my best for Jesus,
> > When He has done so much for me?*

---

*Copyright 1924, renewal 1952 by Harry N. Storrs. Assigned to Singspiration, Inc. Arr. © 1967 by Singspiration, Inc. All rights reserved. Used by permission.

She did not know, nor could she know, that as she sang her song, I sat next door and listened through the wall. I listened to her old, frail voice as she sang her melodic wondering. She was a servant, serving God and His people, like the women on their knees in the prayer room; like her husband and son upstairs pushing a heavy buffer over floors that they willed to shine. I sat, a young man eavesdropping on how to serve God while Mrs. Berryman taught me as she scrubbed toilets and sang. She would not be deterred from the task; she was totally consumed and commissioned to serve, enthralled with the wonder of serving God, and driven by the haunting doubt of whether she was doing enough.

When I woke early this morning, I heard Mrs. Berryman singing again, plain as day. I hadn't heard her song in over twenty years, but I heard the words of Mrs. Berryman's song: "I wonder? Have I done my best for Jesus . . ."

And I wondered.

*Cleanse me . . . and I will be clean.*
(Ps. 51:7 NIV)

# ·11·

# The Violence of Life

After our first son was born, my wife and I decided that if we ever had any more children, we would like to go through birthing classes together, so that I could be with Randee in the delivery room. We hadn't done that with Marcus because classes weren't available then. When we discovered Randee was pregnant with our second child, we called and made arrangements to attend birthing classes now offered in our town.

The fog of evening made us hurry up the steps and into the warmth of the local medical clinic. My wife and I walked into a carpeted room, pillows tucked under our arms. A smiling lady greeted us with name tags, and asked us to have a seat on the floor next to several other couples with pillows. We sat on the floor sipping cups of coffee and waiting, like kindergartners on the first day of school, for the smiling lady to begin the class. She would teach us what to expect. She would tell us what we needed to do. All of the couples sitting on the floor with their pillows were expecting babies, and she would teach us about the wonder of birth. That was more than eighteen years ago . . . and I still remember.

The lady was pleasant—almost too pleasant. She talked of labor, placentas, and episiotomies. She mentioned gowns and gloves and delivery rooms. She described contractions and discomfort. She drew a diagram on the blackboard of what she said was "nature's way of expelling a baby through the birth canal." She talked about how important the father is as a coach and an encourager in this process of birth. But she never talked of pain. "They are not labor pains," she said. "They are contractions."

The birth classes we attended were filled with pretending. Women pretended they were having contractions. They practiced blowing and breathing and panting. The lady teaching the class said that would be helpful when the real birth happened. But until then, the women just *pretended* to have contractions and *practiced* their breathing patterns. Fathers pretended, too. I pretended my wife was having contractions. I timed the imaginary "waves of discomfort" that the lady in front of the class described and encouraged my wife to blow and breathe and pant. But that was sitting on the floor of a carpeted room in a local clinic more than a month before our baby was due. No one was actually *having* a baby in that room, at that moment. We who sat on the floor were *pretending*.

Four weeks later, however, there was no pretending.

Randee looked peaceful and calm as I sat next to her in the labor room of the hospital. We had arrived early that morning, and the doctor had induced labor. We didn't say much at first. Small talk seemed unnecessary and almost unwelcome. But it wasn't long before *they* started. They weren't pains, of course; they were contractions. The "waves of slight discomfort and tightness" had begun. I knew my job, because I'd been practicing. I was responsible for helping my wife focus on something other than "nature's way of expelling a child." I helped her concentrate on her breathing patterns and timed the contractions. They were ten minutes apart.

Then nine . . .

Then eight . . .

I would not describe what my wife was experiencing as "an uncomfortable tightness," as the lady in our classes predicted. *Uncomfortable* is such a civil word, so mild and nondescript. *Uncomfortable* describes a shirt with a scratchy collar or the weather when the humidity is a little too high. It doesn't come close to describing the interminable "waves of contractions" my wife was enduring.

When the contractions reached three-minute intervals, we somehow got stuck. We didn't move from the three minute mark for a long time. The nurse would occasionally come into the room to examine Randee, while I waited outside the door. The nurse always had the same look in her eyes as she came out of the room—like the lady in the birthing classes. "Coming along nicely," she would say.

But Randee said she didn't *feel* like it was coming along nicely. She told me it felt like it was taking forever. It seemed like the eternity of a contraction was separated by three brief minutes, three brief moments to regroup and focus before another eternity of pain began. And all the while, the baby proceeded inexorably down the birth canal.

At about one o'clock in the afternoon, the doctor came in again. He had been in the hospital all morning, but I hadn't seen him until now. He was dressed in his green operating-room gown, green paper boots and hat. The contractions were coming closer together now; it was almost time. The doctor asked me to leave the room and I waited outside while he examined my wife. Within moments, however, the door to the room banged open, and he told me to get dressed in my gown and boots, because we were "going in," he said.

After I got into my garb, I joined my wife, two nurses, and the doctor in the delivery room. I took my place at Randee's head. I coached and held her hand . . . and prayed softly. The doctor performed flawlessly . . . cool and calm, as if he had done this a thousand times before. The contractions seemed nearly constant, now. Randee struggled to expel the child. After one particularly difficult moment, she sighed and said, "I'm trying, doctor, but I can't push. I guess I just can't do this."

I will never forget his reply. He patted her on the foot, and said, "Dearie, you're the only game in town. There's only one person in this room who is going to have a baby, and it's you. If you don't do it, it won't get done." He walked around the delivery room, waiting for another contraction. I sat, holding Randee's hand, telling her how great she was doing. But this was difficult, very difficult.

At the next contraction, the doctor took his position and began using a stern, serious voice. "Now, push with all your might," he commanded. She did. She pushed and groaned and expelled a bloody, blue, writhing human being. The nurses squealed their approval for a job well done.

The doctor spoke again, this time with a sense of pronouncement in his voice. "He's all boy," he said, as he held our son in his gloved hands for a brief moment before placing him on my wife's abdomen. Now, the doctor flashed surgical steel scissors and clamps. Without ceremony, he severed the umbilical tether between mother and son and handed the child to nurses who stood waiting nearby.

I thought to myself, *This must be a violent experience for one so small, one used to the warmth of a womb.* Somehow, I had not expected a birthing room filled with bright lights and cold steel tables. Even though I had been told what to expect, I had not anticipated the stark sights and sounds of birth—green-clad nurses with masks, scissors and clamps and mucous being sucked from nostrils.

I cried. I could not help myself. I cried, as the nurses wiped and measured and examined our new son, polishing him like a trophy just won by an athlete. "Does he have a name?" one of them asked.

I choked back emotion, and said, "Yes. Yes, he has a name. His name is Nathan."

That was nineteen years ago. Nineteen years ago today, Nathan, whose name means *gift of God* came to live in our home. And the experience was one of the most violent I have ever witnessed.

For birthing is a desperate act, you know. When a new life is expelled into light of day, the sights and sounds and pain of that violence defy description. There can be no birthing, no blessed event without interminable pain. There could be no Nathan—no *gift of God* without an ultimate effort: one, final, violent push that purged the womb and rudely introduced his new life into the world.

So it is with rebirth. You may have heard it taught. You may have read books about it. You may have even gone to church and listened as pastors and teachers explained it—how to be born again.

But hearing it described is not the same as experiencing it. The act of rebirth is far more than an uncomfortable tightness of the soul. It is a violent overthrow of sin and self. It is a final severing of the tether of the past, an enabling that allows the new man to know a new and living way. And this introduction, this rebirthing, this gift of God flows from and goes far beyond any mortal man or woman's ability to accomplish.

It takes Another—One who faced interminable pain to bring Eternal Life.

> *... the gift of God is eternal life in Christ Jesus our Lord.*
> (Rom. 6:23)

# ·12·

# The Key of A

Our house has been filled with music since my wife and I were first married. We love music of all kinds, and as our family has grown, and sons have been added to our home, the style (and volume) of the music we listened to changed and broadened and enlarged. But I have noticed that there is more than one *kind* of music.

One kind comes from outside—through radio, or tapes or CDs. It's music that someone else makes up for you and plays at your command. Another kind of music is the music created within the home—played by family members who practice trumpet, or guitar or drums, sharing their gift or talent with those around them.

But a third kind of music is what this story is about. This kind of music resonates with a *felt* melody, not necessarily sung or played. It's music acted out by the soul, a tune hummed deep within the spirit; an attitude that says, "O what a beautiful morning; O what a beautiful day...."

My son Simeon has had that kind of music playing in his life ever since he was little. He makes his brothers laugh as he acts and jokes and plays the song of his life. It is a happy, unencumbered song. But the year of his seventh grade in school, without warning or apparent cause, he stopped singing that song.

His mother noticed it first. The normal light in his eyes, she said—the glint of sun in her son that was always there—wasn't. She mentioned it to me. "Have you noticed Simeon, lately? He's not his usual, joyful self. He seems to be 'down' about something. He complains about headaches, too."

"Oh, I don't know," I said. "I don't notice anything different. Maybe it's just a stage he's going through." But after she mentioned it, I *did* begin to notice. And what I noticed caused me some concern.

Simeon usually lilts along as he walks, as if he actually has somewhere important to go. It's not a fast step, but the bounce and cadence of his walk brings with it a surety that he is happy. Gradually, however, I noticed melancholy creep into his manner. I talked to Simeon about his spirit and asked him if he was all right. I asked about the headaches, too. Did he think it was his eyes?

Simeon didn't say very much. He didn't like school this year, he said. It seemed that all he ever got to do was go to school, come home and eat, and then do two to two-and-a-half hours of homework—every night. He said he felt he was under a lot of pressure. So I scheduled a meeting with all of his teachers one day after school.

When I walked into the meeting room, the teachers sat in a semicircle around a chair they had obviously prepared for me. As I sat down, they all smiled and one of them thanked me for coming. As she talked, I couldn't help but tune her out for just a moment. Inside, where the teachers could not see, I grimaced as my nerves felt the pinch of an old feeling I hadn't had in years—a feeling that comes when you sit before teachers with grade books; a feeling reminiscent of fear and failure.

They all had grade books on their laps. This meeting was about Simeon Jones, so of course all of them had turned to the page called "Simeon." They were prepared. They anticipated my asking them how he was doing in school. They readied themselves for a reading of the litany—grades and numbers and red marks. I'm sure it all must have been there: the record, the evidence, the proof of how he did or didn't pay attention in math, how he had done poorly on his science project, or that he seemed to be doing well in English, but he talked to his friend Bob much too much. If I had asked them, they would have given me every missing assignment, days absent, tardies, and tests, . . . and trivia. But I was determined to avoid a trivial pursuit.

"Thank you all for coming," I began. "I've come to talk to you about Simeon. I look to you as fellow members of an educational team. My wife and I support your efforts, and we want you to know how much we appreciate all you're doing for Simeon. I see that you have come prepared to talk about Sim's academic progress, but you can all put your books away, because this meeting is not about his grades. We say almost nothing about grades at our house. This meeting is not about reading or science; it's not about math or history. It's about music. I've been listening for Simeon's song, and it seems to have gone away. I was just wondering if any of you would have any idea why his heart stopped singing . . . and how can we encourage him to begin the song again?"

Relief gave a sigh. Dialogue relaxed. Interrogation walked out of the room. "Why did you give my kid a bad grade" never showed up. There was no need for documentation, for nothing was being questioned in regard to their performance. Instead, a search for answers started.

We spent almost an hour, wondering and talking about my son—and his song—not his grades. And as we speculated and conversed, patterns began to emerge. We committed ourselves to cooperation between school and home and to a determination not to let the song stop. A circle was formed by teachers and parents to inspire and encourage and . . . care about the music in another's soul.

I'll not bore you with the details of our plan for Simeon that day. Suffice it to say we "tricked" him—tricks-of-the-trade, you might say. It's quite a trick to convince a child in this pressure-packed, competitive society that grades or accomplishments do not define a person's worth or character. It didn't happen in a few days, or even a few weeks, but eventually Simeon's song returned. All he really needed, I suppose, was our permission to find fulfillment in something besides "A"s.

He's like me, I guess. Always straining to reach those high notes in the key of A gives me a horrific headache.

*Serve the LORD with gladness;*
*Come before His presence with singing.*
(Ps. 100:2)

# ·13·

# The Mourning After

*I will hide the identity of the characters in this true saga so that you may know the story, but not the people who lived it. You must never know who they are. God knows them and how much they have suffered, and that is enough.*

The knock on the pastor's front door could not have come at a more inconvenient time. His wife had been after him for weeks to finish the job, and wet wallpaper wrapped itself around his arm as he stood on a chair next to his wife trying to get the sticky paper into position.

Another knock . . . and a ring of the doorbell. He stepped off his chair-scaffold, wiped the glue from his arms and hands, and answered the door. He recognized the woman who greeted him. She was a single parent who lived in his neighborhood, a Catholic woman who mistakenly called him "Father" sometimes when she saw him in the grocery store.

"I'm so sorry to bother you, Father, but I don't know what else to do. Can we talk for a moment, please?" He invited her in, and as they walked into the living room, the quiver in her voice made him know that something awful had happened. The pastor offered her a seat on the couch, and his wife brought her a glass of water to help her regain her composure.

"How can I help you?" he finally asked.

"It's my daughter. I've found out something about her today. She's only fourteen, and . . . I don't know what to do." She looked into her lap and started to sob.

Except for the sound of the woman's sorrow, the only noise the pastor could hear was the stillness of his own inner voice. Sometimes when people talked to him—told him their story—his *thinking* raced to the end of their story before they had a chance to reveal all of the plot. Sometimes his lame brain made up its own mind about where a story was headed and ran to the end of the street, waiting for the storyteller to catch up.

That's the way it was this time. He already knew what she was going to say. He'd heard stories like this one a thousand times. His thoughts began to shape the woman's halting story before she could even say the words. *Pregnant,* he thought, as he listened to the sobbing woman. *I'll bet she found out her daughter is pregnant.*

But as the woman regained control of her emotions and continued her story, he could tell it wasn't *that.* She talked about finding something in a dresser drawer. *Drugs,* he thought. *I've heard this before. I'll bet she was putting away some clean clothes and she found some drugs in one of her daughter's dresser drawers.*

"When I saw it, I couldn't believe it was really her," she said. "Seeing her like that made me sick at my stomach."

*Wait a minute,* the pastor thought. *She's not talking about drugs, and she's not talking about a pregnancy.* "What did you find that upset you so much?" he asked. And this time he didn't let his mind run to the end of the street or finish the woman's sentence for her. Instead, he listened.

"This," she said, as she pulled a picture from an envelope in her hand. It was a picture of her fourteen-year-old daughter, nude and sitting on a couch. "I recognize the couch," she said. "It belongs to Jim and Martha, our neighbor friends across the street. I also found this." She handed the pastor the rest of the contents of the envelope. It was a letter written by Jim to her daughter—a love letter, filled with numerous details of sexual intimacy. The pastor knew now why the mother felt sick. He felt sick, too.

The woman broke down again and sobbed. The pastor's wife sat beside her, held her, comforted her. Finally, after a few more moments, the woman continued her story. She had known the couple across the street for about three years. The woman said that after her husband died, the neighbor couple befriended her and her daughter. The man managed a local grocery store chain, and his wife—a nice lady who worked nights—seemed to go out of her way to extend friendship to this single mom and her only child. The two families went on vacations together. They water-skied and had picnics together. The mother had no idea anything like this was going on. But now, as she pieced together the details of the letter and the picture of the young girl, a sickening story unfolded.

Each evening the young girl, a freshman in high school, would help her mother by starting dinner. After the evening meal, the girl would watch a little television and then spend one or two hours on homework. About ten o'clock, she would take her shower and go to bed. After her mother had retired for the evening—and after Martha, the nice lady who lived across the street, had driven off into the night to go to work—the young girl would open the back window of her bedroom, crawl quietly out, and make her way across the street to spend the night with Jim. In the early hours of morning, she would re-trace her steps and crawl back through the window of her bedroom—before her mother got up and before Martha returned home from her night of work.

The pastor and his wife prayed with the woman and did their best to comfort her before she finally went home. The next morning, the pastor sat with the woman as she called the local child protective agency. He sat with her later that day, too, when an investigator from the agency came to the woman's home and interviewed her and her daughter. The pastor chilled at the glacial looks of the uncooperative child of fourteen. She seemed detached, he thought, and distant.

"The law is pretty clear about these kinds of things," the man told the mother. "Be assured that action will be taken," he said.

After the investigator left, the pastor talked with the woman and her daughter for a few more minutes before he told them he must go. He told the mother he would come back anytime if she needed him.

She did. She needed him about four-thirty that afternoon.

"Can you come now? I really need some help," the mother said to the pastor on the phone. "Martha is here—Jim's wife. I don't know what Jim said to her, but she's standing on the sidewalk in front of our house right now. She's very belligerent and angry, and she wants to know what's going on. The police must have called Jim at work and told him about the investigation, because he came home early. I think my daughter may have called him, too. Martha insists on talking with my daughter, and I don't know what to do."

The pastor drove the two blocks to her house, wondering what he would find when he got there.

As he pulled up to the house, the mother and her daughter stood on the sidewalk, while a few feet away another woman stood—Martha, he supposed—a stern, angry look on her face. The pastor got out of his car and walked toward the three people. As he approached, the mother introduced him to the woman. "Father, this is Martha, our neighbor from across the street."

The pastor smiled at the angry-looking woman, trying to appear friendly and non-threatening. It was obvious that she knew something about her husband's involvement with the young girl now, and he could not possibly imagine her pain or confusion at this moment. He introduced himself and reached to shake her hand.

She responded with raw anger. "Who do you think you are?" she said to the pastor, as she glared at his extended hand. Her arms remained folded and closed across her chest, protecting her broken heart.

"Oh, I'm just a pastor who cares," said the pastor as he strategized what to do next.

"Can we use your living room to sit down and talk?" he said to the mother. She nodded in relief. The pastor led the way and, with some reluctance, Martha followed the mother and her child into their home. Four of the characters in this tragic drama would now sit and talk about the discoveries and disclosures of the past twenty-four hours.

Across the street, Jim must have watched from his living room window. He decided. As soon as he saw them enter the house, he *knew*. He knew what his wife heard across the street. He knew what the police had said to him that day on the phone. He knew there would be an investigation, interviews, evidence . . . and shame.

He couldn't stop it.

But he couldn't face it, either.

So, while his wife sat in a living room across the street listening to a story that would shatter her life, Jim walked out into the backyard and ended his. He walked into the light of the late afternoon sun, and he left this world. He stuck the barrel of a twelve-gauge shotgun in his mouth and made his last tragic decision.

The next three hours blurred with sights and sounds too horrible to describe and too graphic to ever forget. The pastor tried to console those who were inconsolable. He found himself walking from person to person, trying to speak, but realizing . . . that he did not know what to say.

He did not know what to say to the broken-hearted mother whose daughter had been so deceived and violated by a trusted neighbor and friend.

He had no words for the fourteen-year-old child who cursed him because he would not allow her to go across the street to see her "friend" Jim.

He stood nearly speechless, trying to comfort the wife—a wife who thought she was furious enough to kill her husband because he had betrayed her—until she ran across the street and into their backyard and discovered that he had already taken care of that. She looked off into nothingness, a shocked, blank stare on her face and a hollow reality in her soul. She did not know what to do with this awfulness.

But He knew. God, who is the First and Last and final Word, knew that there are some scars so deep, some wounds so grievous that they cannot be soothed with mere, mortal words. These three women—all betrayed by the same man in a different way—needed the Man of Sorrows, the One who suffered the ultimate betrayal. And they needed time.

Healing did come to them. Slowly, and with the help of pastors and counselors and supportive friends, the Healer brought the balm of healing and hope to their lives.

Why did such a tragedy happen?

Like Job of old, they still do not know *why*. They only know that life's unfathomable meanings and explanations are best left to Him.

For, He who brings all things to pass in His *own* time—He who will one day speak and say, "Enough! No *more* time"—that same God is also faithful to bring solace and comfort to those weeping of heart . . . in the meantime.

*Blessed are those who mourn,*
*For they shall be comforted.*
(Matt. 5:4)

# ·14·

# Junior High Chapel

In the middle of the Great Central Valley of California there is a growing, clean, not-too-fancy, not-too-plain town. Forty acres of peach trees sit on the northern outskirts of that town, where peaches hang heavy and ripe as the August heat softens and sweetens them.

Quiet reigns in that orchard during most of June, July, and August. Forty acres of peaches are very quiet when they grow. Some gray buildings stand in the middle of the orchard. The buildings are stark, plain and vacant of life during the searing summer heat.

But September brings noise to the orchard. It always does. Sounds of laughter and hellos fill the air. Junior high school students have come to this campus in the middle of a peach orchard, bringing with them the smell of new jeans and never-before-worn shirts, carrying empty book bags that would bulge with texts by day's end. It was the first day of a new school year.

I had been invited to speak at their opening-day chapel, for this was a Christian school, and chapel was an important part of their weekly education. The stares as I walked down the sidewalk toward the chapel told me that some of them were wondering about me. *Was I a new math teacher? Or maybe a history teacher?* I smiled and nodded as I passed giggly girls who had grown six inches over the summer, and serious boys who hadn't.

I walked to the room where chapel would be held—an ordinary room, with an upright piano in the corner. Brown stains had replaced the ivory on several keys of the old piano, and when I tried it, I heard that the long, hot summer had sapped the tuning from its strings. There were only a few chairs scattered around the edges of this room, and I wondered what the seating for chapel would be like. But I didn't wonder for long.

The bell rang at precisely 8:15 A.M. A few moments later, the doors to the room opened, and people with grade books and stern looks—obviously the teachers—oversaw the orderly march of kids into the room. Having once been a teacher myself, I was familiar with the "game face" that teachers don the first few days of school to show the kids who's in charge.

The students entered the room totally oblivious to everything around them except each other and sat down on the floor, some of them reclining on their elbows, others sitting up straight. The teachers all sat in the chairs around the edge of the room, their eyes scanning the crowd of one-hundred-or-so bobbing heads that never stopped talking.

The room quieted when the principal walked to the front of the group. While he made his This-is-the-first-day-of-the-rest-of-your-life speech (which, by the way, hasn't changed much since *I* was in junior high school), I scanned this group for signs of life—not biological life . . . spiritual life. Who were these kids? And what did they need to hear? I was accustomed to talking to adults. I was used to talking to people whose backs would be breaking if they sat on the floor like these kids.

I had prepared a little talk about faith or beginnings or some such tiresome topic that these kids had heard before. As the principal finished his speech and began my introduction, I could see the kids eyeing me—deciding if they liked me, deciding if they were going to listen.

I made a decision of my own at that moment. I decided to take a risk.

The students applauded politely as I walked to the front. I took a small New Testament from my coat, and ignoring the notes I had scribbled on a piece of paper, I read a very familiar text: "For where two or three are gathered together in My name, I am there in the midst of them" (Matt. 18:20).

I began with a simple question: "How many of you believe that statement?" Predictably, the room raised its collective hand. I would not have expected any different. These were "Christian" kids, with "Christian" teachers, at a "Christian" school. They most likely attended church regularly, and they knew all the right answers. They stood when it was time to stand in church and sat when it was time to sit. They knew all the right phrases and could speak "Christianese" with flawless diction. And they most certainly knew when a rhetorical question was being asked—and how to answer it—without really thinking.

I walked around to the front of the lectern and pointed to the redheaded boy in the front row.

"If I gave this young man—What's your name, pal?"

"Jason."

"If I took out a nickel, gave it to Jason, and told him it was half of what I have left in my pocket, how much did I have when I started?"

In every room full of people, there tend to be two basic types: those who hold back and those who rush ahead. A girl with long, blonde hair spoke out, like people who know the answer always do.

"Ten cents," she said. Her friend sitting next to her smiled, congratulating her on her quick math computation.

"Thanks." I pointed toward the blonde girl and acknowledged her answer. I continued, as I walked back and forth in front of the students now.

"The verse I just read seems to indicate that wherever two or three people gather in the name of Christ, He is there, too. And all of you agreed with that statement. It's nice when we can be so unanimous about something, isn't it?" They didn't have a clue about *why* I was asking that question, but because I nodded my head as I asked it, they all nodded back, as if their heads were attached to an imaginary string, like marionettes.

I decided that the girl in the second row on the right—the one wearing new tennis shoes with purple laces—would be next.

"If I took out a nickel, gave it to you, and told you it was half of what I have left in my pocket . . . how much did I have when I started?"

"Ten cents." She looked down as she answered, smiling a bit.

"Excellent," I said. "Thanks for the answer."

The adults in the chairs around the edge of the room looked puzzled as I walked back and forth across the front. Their "game-faces" had slipped a bit, and some of them were having difficulty getting them readjusted, as they tried to determine where I was heading with this line of questioning.

"There are some things," I said, "which are just so obvious we don't even have to think about them, aren't there?" The room full of marionettes nodded their heads, as I nodded mine.

"And when we hear certain questions or comments that we've heard before, we don't even have to think about the answers, do we?" Now, I slowly shook my head no, and like lemmings on their way to the sea, the students followed the leader.

"And when I ask you if you believe that where two or three are gathered in Christ's name, He is there, too, what would you say?"

The big guy sitting toward the back—probably a football player—was next, and I pointed to him.

"What would you say? Do you *really* believe that?"

"Yes." A serious reply and certain. No question about it, the football player knew the right answer.

"And would you say we are gathered here today in Christ's name?"

"Yes." The camera was still on the football player.

"So you would say you *believe* Christ is here in spirit?"

"Yes." Not long answers, but safe, because he was sure he was right.

*Time for a show of hands*, I thought.

"How many of you agree with him, that we are gathered here in the name of Christ?" I raised my hand as I asked the question, and now everyone in the room raised their hand, too.

"And how many of you *really believe* that Jesus is here in spirit because we have gathered in His name?" The hands still remained raised.

"And one more quick question. How many of you agree that if I gave you a nickel and said this is half of what I have left in my pocket, I must have had a dime to start with?"

Everyone in the room was caught-up in the frenzy of the moment. They all held their hands high, certain of the answer.

All but one.

The math teacher put his hand down when I asked the last question. Because he was sitting in the back, none of the students noticed he put his hand down. But I noticed. In fact, I counted on it.

"I'm almost finished talking. Thanks for being patient with me and letting me come to your chapel." The looks on their faces told me they were totally confused. I had only spoken three minutes, and I was ready to conclude?

"Sometimes, when we are faced with an obvious truth, we can arrive at the answer without really thinking about the process. We sort of throw our minds into auto-pilot and get comfortable with an answer because we know it's right. That's what most of you did this morning. You fell into a trap because your brains were on auto-pilot. And I let you do it in the hope that it will make you think."

The math teacher in the back smiled, now, and his was the solitary head that nodded in understanding. I pointed to him and asked my ten-cent question.

"If I gave you a nickel, told you it was half of all I have left in my pocket, how much did I have when I started?"

"Fifteen cents!" he said. "You had fifteen cents when you started."

The room erupted in talk, as students tried desperately to argue with the math teacher. He continued to smile, arms folded, legs stretched out in a comfortable position. He *knew* he was right, and he knew exactly *why* he was right. Before total chaos rained down on my presentation, I spoke.

"All of you gave the wrong answer—ten cents. It wasn't a *bad* answer. In fact, ten cents would have been a great answer if I had said, 'Here's a nickel; it's half of all I've got. How much do I have?' But that was not the question I asked, now was it?"

They tried to recall the exact question, but no one volunteered. Now they were listening to every word, not wanting to miss the point again.

"What I said was, 'Here's a nickel. It's half of all I have *left in my pocket.* That means I must have a dime left in my pocket, plus the nickel I'm giving you. So I had fifteen cents when I started! Your answers were automatic answers, but they were incorrect because you failed to *listen* when the question was asked, and you answered a question that *wasn't* asked."

The gangly-legged students sitting in front of me had no idea why I had started their first chapel of the year with a silly, meaningless math problem. But I thought they had heard enough of me. Now they needed to think some more.

"I'll give you one more chance. Imagine with me that today, as the principal introduced the guest speaker, it wasn't me. It was Jesus. You said you really believe He is in the midst of any two or three gathered in His name. Imagine with me, will you? After you said your pledge to the flag and the announcements were made, imagine that the principal said, 'And now, ladies and gentlemen, Jesus is coming through the back door—our guest speaker for the day.'"

I took some risk, now. I walked over to the old upright piano and sat down on its bench. I looked straight into their eyes and said, "If you saw Him coming through the back door . . . what would you do?" They could tell that automatic, mindless answers wouldn't do this time. I was serious. And I intended to wait until they responded.

It was quiet in the room, now, quiet as peaches growing. But after several moments of silence, a young man near the front spoke. He said rather timidly, "I'd ask Him how He was doing."

I smiled, and nodded. But I said nothing. This was *their* sermon now.

Many more seconds passed, before a pretty little girl, popular I supposed, spoke as she raised her hand. "I'd ask Him if He wanted to eat lunch with us girls." For some reason, that statement broke the dike of hesitancy, and comments started coming in a regular, rhythmic pattern—profound, incredible, like-a-child comments that were innocent and open and honest.

One rather frail-looking boy with horn-rimmed glasses spoke up. "I'd ask Him if He liked to play chess." And still another: "I'd ask Him if He wanted to come to our pep rally at noon today."

After perhaps four or five minutes of students wondering what it would be like to invite the Invisible Guest into the most common and ordinary moments of their lives, things became quiet again. I thought chapel was nearly over. I thought wrong.

For near the back door of the room sat one boy, somewhat separated from the rest, and not with any particular group of students. He had a pensive face, and it seemed to me he was about to speak. He did not. Instead, he stood.

He was the only person in the room who stood. He looked to the front, took a deep breath, and then started applauding. His eyes of faith had caught a glimpse of the Guest of honor, and he stood to his feet with an ovation—alone; vulnerable; incredible.

Within moments, the entire student body of that junior high school was standing, joining in the clapping and smiling and honoring the Risen One who had come to chapel. But they weren't following the leader; they were following the Leader.

We couldn't see Him, but I know He was there. He said He would come when a group of His kids got together. He stood in the middle of that classroom, in the middle of that campus, in the middle of an orchard of soft, sweet, growing peaches, and soft, sweet, growing children.

And He smiled.

*. . . whoever does not receive the kingdom of God*
*as a little child*
*will by no means enter it.*
(Mark 10:15)

# •15•

# Bandit

The snow on Mount Lassen in early summer stands out like a lighthouse beacon against the northern California sky. The mountain overlooks the northern end of the Great Central Valley where we lived. It's hot in that valley in the summertime. It's cool on that mountain, a perfect spot for a week-long vacation. My wife and I decided to pack up our three sons and enjoy the great outdoors.

I love the smell of the mountains, and as we pulled the trailer into our assigned camping spot, my lungs were already enjoying the clean mountain air. Within moments of our arrival, ten-year-old Marcus and his two younger brothers were pounding tent stakes and stretching lines. None of that sissy trailer stuff for them.

Marcus had purchased a new pup-tent with his own money. He and his two brothers would be roughing it by sleeping in the tent.

Bandit sat close-by and watched. Bandit the kitten was three months old—just a baby. He had white, reasonably well-groomed fur, dotted with spots of brown and black.

I'm not the cat lover in our family. I don't *dislike* them, you understand. I'm neutral on cats. My wife and kids, on the other hand, have always loved cats, and this little fellow seemed to fit into the framework of our family. It was only natural that we would include him in our vacation plans.

Randee and I enjoyed listening to our kids work together on the tent, as we began to secure the trailer and unpack. As I was placing wooden blocks under the wheels of the trailer, I noticed a beautiful doe, about fifty yards outside our camp. She didn't seem afraid of people. *Probably the campground mascot,* I thought. The deer seemed particularly interested in the commotion of the boys setting up their tent, and slowly walked over to investigate.

As she approached the outer edges of our campsite, the deer's large, mule-like ears rose, and her nose pointed toward our kitten. Bandit noticed the deer at the same time the deer noticed Bandit. I stopped what I was doing, and called my wife from out of the trailer to watch this cute encounter. Marcus stopped pounding his tent stakes. Nathan and Simeon backed away slowly, and all five of us began to talk in whispered tones, not wanting to frighten the deer. I smiled as I watched my children enjoying this wonderful encounter, and whispered to my wife, "I wish we had the camera ready."

Nose to nose. Like a scene out of *Bambi* the two animals crept toward each other. *This is the kind of thing I hoped my kids could see while we were here,* I thought. *Nothing like the out-of-doors to teach kids the beauty of God's creation.*

But I thought wrong.

As the beautiful deer approached to within two or three feet of our kitten—without warning and without provocation—the doe reared on her hind feet and trounced Bandit with two slashing blows of her front hooves.

It happened quicker than I could have imagined. Totally unexpected, in an instant, tranquillity changed to chaos.

My sons screamed in horror at the sight. They ran to my wife and me, frightened and frantic, hoping we could stop this violent show. The doe did not seem particularly alarmed at their screams, but turned and walked slowly into an adjoining camp while Bandit the kitty flopped and flounced and . . . died.

Randee and I hurried our three sons into the trailer, away from the tragic scene. As my family huddled into a circle around the table in the camper, I tried to gather my thoughts, thoughts that might ease this awful hurt, thoughts about what to say.

But before I spoke, I listened.

I listened to Marcus, and I could hear the anger in his ten-year-old voice, anger directed at the deer. "I should have hit that deer with the hammer I was using to drive those tent stakes," he said. "I didn't know that a deer would kill a baby kitty. I don't like it here, and I want to go home."

Nathan sat next to me, sagging against my side. Silent tears slid down his red face, as he stared at some fixed point in the corner of the room. The voiceless pain in Nathan's eight-year-old face was so evident that I could almost hear it. He didn't speak, but as he leaned against my side, I could feel his pain.

I felt Simeon's pain, too. He was the youngest, only five. But as he sat on his mother's lap crying, he had profound questions. As Randee rocked him and tried to calm him, he probed for answers. "I don't like deers no more. Why are they so mean, Dad? Why did that deer kill my kitty?"

Three sets of solemn eyes looked my direction and waited for me to speak. I couldn't think of anything to say, but like most pastors, I have the ability to talk until I *do* think of something to say. I held my wife's hand for assurance and began. "I'm very sorry about what happened to Bandit. I didn't know that the deer would hurt our kitty. Cats and deer are natural enemies in the wild. The deer didn't know the difference between a baby bobcat and a domestic cat and was probably just trying to protect herself."

That's a thumbnail sketch of what took me about twenty minutes to say—scientific, analytical, an attempted explanation of the inexplicable. In that small trailer on top of that mountain, I talked and talked . . . but I'm not convinced that what I had to say to my kids was what they needed to hear. I hurt for my kids, and my wife and I tried to comfort them. But I struggled trying to explain *death* to three kids who were all too young to understand *life*.

We survived the week in the mountains. On the way back home we stopped to see my wife's folks, who live on a farm with cats . . . and kittens. When my boys told their grandpa what the deer had done, he went out to the barn. He handpicked a terrific kitten about three months old—Bandit II. Grandpa told my children that they could have this kitty to replace the one that died. I thank God for grandpas.

I wanted my kids to be exposed to the wonders of God's creation on our trip . . . and they were. Life taught them something I couldn't. They were having a mountaintop experience until life walked into the midst of their plans and left death as a calling card. But death didn't stay: a new life was prepared out of the ashes of the old.

Don't be surprised at what God allows to come your way. Whether you're on the mountaintop or down in the valley, every day will have some living and some dying and some living again.

> *But thanks be to God! He gives us the victory*
> *through our Lord Jesus Christ.*
> (1 Cor. 15:57 NIV)

# ·16·

# They Say San Diego Is Lovely This Time of Year

If you call my house the week after next, we won't be home. We have to go to San Diego. My wife and I and our three sons plan to make the trip in two cars. We'll have to rent a trailer, because of all the stuff. They say San Diego is lovely this time of year. I know he'll enjoy it . . . Marcus, I mean. For you see, in just a few weeks, Marcus—my first son, my oldest child, my very good friend—leaves for college, and he won't be coming back . . . at least not to stay.

He will begin a new life as a university student. I think he was wise to attend the local community college after he graduated from high school. His mother and I were glad to have him continue living here at home for these last two years while he got some of his basic course work out of the way. But now, he's transferring to a university to finish his degree. He's made arrangements for an apartment, and he and his mother are already packing and planning how to decorate. I occasionally hear them talking about towels and curtains and bedspreads. He's going to take some stuff from our house to set up his new place: a bed and dresser, a couple of lamps, some dishes and pots and pans. My wife has been setting small appliances aside for months: an old vacuum, a toaster, an iron, and a blender with instructions taped to its side—*Works just fine, but you have to jiggle the switch.* It's apparent—to this parent—that Marcus plans a longer stay in San Diego. He's setting up house. He's intent on making a permanent home for himself—a permanent home away from *home.*

I never realized that so much emotion was attached to "things." I didn't know that taking pictures off the wall could produce such strong feelings; deep, mixed moods; both melancholy and maudlin. I don't know how everyone else in the family feels about Marcus leaving home, but for me, it's not easy.

Nate's the next oldest. He will soon wear the mantle of "the oldest son in the house." Does that feel strange to him? I don't know, but before Marcus leaves, I plan to ask Nathan how he feels about that.

I'll probably ask Simeon, too. His oldest brother has been his pal and model and friend. What's it feel like to have your oldest brother gather up his belongings and stack them in a corner ready to be loaded into a trailer? When I get the chance, I think I'll ask Sim.

Randee's the momma, of course, and she must feel like a mother. I have no idea what *that* feels like—but I do talk to her some about it, and she tries to tell me how she feels. When she talks, there is a mother-pain that I hear. It's a "birthing" pain that only mothers can know, I think: a pain that first comes when babies are finally born after nine long months of waiting; a pain that comes again when those same "babies" separate themselves from their mothers a second time. Joy and expectation mix with sorrow and anguish to form a bittersweet cup. The marrow of a mother's heart cannot be separated from her own flesh and blood. But Randee seems to be facing this rebirth of her oldest child with braveness and a genuine sense of expectancy.

No, I don't know what the other members of my family *feel* about the oldest brother and child and friend leaving home. But I know what I feel.

I guess the biggest thing I'm dealing with as I contemplate my son's departure is the *wondering*. Try as I might, I can't keep my mind from opening the door of "I wonder if..." and then walking into a room filled with all sorts of scary things. Some of the things that scare me are pragmatic, important, visible things that can be touched and seen and felt.

What's he going to do if he runs out of money before he runs out of month?

He doesn't have a job yet. Where's he going to work? What if he can't find a job?

What if he gets sick?

What if he stops going to church?

What if he can't find a good friend?

What if he *does* find a . . . girl friend?

I try not to spend too much time with those types of wanderings and wonderings, however. They all tend to focus on the future, and of course, I know I have no control over his future. But I *have* had some control on his past. There is a gnawing that eats away at my inner dad-self; hope and fear and doubt all wrapped tightly into one package that I'm almost afraid to open: *Have I told him everything? Did I forget anything? What more does he need to know about life before he walks out my front door toward a front door of his own?*

It occurs to me that reading about someone else's child leaving home may be a little bit like looking at the family pictures in someone else's wallet. They're nice pictures, but they're not yours. You don't have strong feelings about the people pictured in someone else's wallet. And you may not feel anything at all as I tell you about my son—my oldest son who's going away to make a life of his own, away from his brothers; away from his mother and his dad and his home.

But you'll feel it if it ever happens to you.

I don't know *what* you will feel exactly, because all families are different. But I am convinced that reality will set in as you pack up the boxes.

If you're like my wife and me, then you'll be packing prayers with the toaster. You'll be tucking in your very best wishes with the dish rags and towels. And in spite of all you can do, you won't be able to resist. You'll take every opportunity as the day of leaving approaches to impart some final thought; some pearl of wisdom, some "don't-forget-to . . .", some last minute instructions to reinforce what you hope you've said earlier in life. Then, you'll load the car, as I will the week after next. You'll take a quiet drive to your own "San Diego." And the ride back home will be quieter, still.

I have come to a new understanding and appreciation of a sacred, solemn trust-agreement between the Lord God in heaven and parents on earth. I have known all along that children are a gift of God, a loan of love. It's just that I didn't fully appreciate a reality that has been true from the very beginning: Children come to pass . . . but they don't come to stay.

*Sons are a heritage from the LORD,*
*children a reward from him.*
(Ps. 127:3 NIV)

# ·17·

# The Apartment

*W*eariness. *More than weariness. Exhaustion.* I sat in a van looking out on the waterfront of Amsterdam. The musicians I had taken to Europe for seven weeks slept in contorted positions in the back of the van, having spent nearly eleven hours on the road. It was almost midnight. Through bleary eyes I watched the huge cargo ships slide through the channel, as I remembered our recent weeks of travel and concerts. We had been singing on military bases throughout Europe, trying to bring the Good News to some of the loneliest people in the world—U.S. military personnel and their families overseas.

We were almost finished with the tour now, and it felt good to have arrived in Amsterdam after such a long trip and to know that rest and sleep were only minutes away. Our friends who lived on a barge on the water's edge had invited us to spend the night. I looked forward to taking advantage of their hospitality.

*Hope. More than hope. Expectation.* I watched as a young man came off the barge and made his way over to our van. In a touching expression of genuine Christian love, he extended his hand through the window, smiled and said, "Velcome!"

He described our sleeping arrangements. "The barge is very crowded, but I think vee vill be able to sleep all of you. But vee have no beds. You vill have to sleep on the deck."

*Anxiety. More than anxiety. Fear.* One of the six sleeping passengers in the back of the van was my wife. Pregnant with our second child, she had been a real trooper on this trip. She hadn't asked for any special treatment during our entire trek, even though our living conditions had been less than ideal. But now, the thought of subjecting her to a night on the deck of a bobbing barge after an eleven hour trip in a bouncing van caused me to worry for my wife and for our unborn child.

*Important. More than important. Urgent.* "Please, sir. My wife is in the back, and she is expecting a child. I am concerned for her welfare. Is there any way we could get her a bed?" He looked like a merchant marine, as he stood leaning on the van, his dark navy wool hat pulled down around his ears. His large hand stroked his beard of stubbled whiskers, and he seemed pensive and serious for a moment. He peeked through the window to see my sleeping passengers and then patted my arm. "Vee shall see vhat vee kahn do," he said in a broken English accent, as he smiled and disappeared up the gangway. Somehow, I felt he would be able to oblige my request.

---

**Like sleepy children marching to the drumbeat of bedtime, they followed, one behind the other up the gangplank and into the bowels of the barge . . .**

---

In a few moments, he returned and said, "Vee vill house everyone but you and your vife here on the barge. Arrangements have been made for an apartment for the two of you. Please have your friends get their things and follow me. I'll be back in a few minutes to take you and your vife to the apartment."

The unconscious souls in the back of the van began to stir and unceremoniously gathered their overnight bags. Like sleepy children marching to the drumbeat of bedtime, they followed, one behind the other up the gangplank and into the bowels of the barge for quick showers and much-needed rest on deck.

*Solitude. More than solitude. Privacy.* The sounds of sleeping people now gone from the van, Randee and I sat in the quiet and wondered about our accommodations for the night. Would we have to pay for the apartment? Would we be sharing it with someone else? How far would we have to drive before we could finally get some rest?

It took nearly half an hour to get everyone settled on the barge—an eternity when you're really tired. But finally, I saw two figures walking down the gangway and approaching our van. A man and a woman opened the door of the van and got in. She said very little, but he explained that there was an apartment available to travelers like my wife and me. He and his wife would take us there, and we could spend the night. The woman got out of our van, and into another car. She would follow us, and her husband would be our guide through the night streets of Amsterdam.

*Eerie. More than eerie. Surreal.* The streets of Amsterdam were lit with a harsh, orange-yellow light that made shadows deepen. We drove to the city's edge, and beyond; out into the Dutch countryside. The bright moonlight revealed pastoral scenes of cows and hay. We could see an occasional windmill, its silhouette painted black and fixed against Holland's sky. The signs on the road marked the way to little hamlets and villages, villages with strange looking names, names that seemed to have too many consonants and not enough vowels to be pronounceable.

After several minutes of riding into the dark countryside, we saw lights in the distance of another town. We approached the little village and turned into what looked in the dark like an apartment complex. Our guide pointed toward a parking spot, and we pulled into a space. We quickly gathered our luggage from the van and made our way toward the door of a two-story building.

*Friends. More than friends. Family.* The building we approached was obviously an apartment building, and we noticed the mail slots next to the front door as we entered its lobby. *One of these kind families will be sharing their home with us tonight,* I thought.

Four doors led to four separate apartments downstairs, with large letters on the doors. Wide stairs were off to the left of the lobby, and our guide pointed to them, and said, "This way." As we walked up the stairs, the smell of someone else's house filled the stairwell, an olfactory reminder that we were entering another's private world. When we reached the top of the stairs, our guide stuck a key in a door, apartment E, and opened it. He stepped aside and motioned us to enter. I gladly walked by him, and into what would be our quarters for the night.

*Old. More than old. Antique.* The clocks and photos and furnishings of this place were an obvious showcase of memories. Lovely, but not fancy, warm, inviting, *velcome* in the truest sense of that word. Our guide showed us through the small apartment and helped me with the luggage. The apartment was immaculate. The sound of clocks ticking formed a chorus of syncopation, each with a different tick, each with a different tock.

Our guide, before leaving us to our rest, told us the story of the old woman who lived in this apartment. She was out of the country right now, he said. She had called him just prior to leaving and asked him to come over.

"I'll be gone for a few weeks and would appreciate your watching my little apartment while I'm away," she had said.

He had agreed.

She asked him to join her in prayer about her apartment and he told us what she prayed. "Lord, I know that while I am gone, You will want to use this place to bring rest and comfort to weary children of Yours. Please direct them here, and may they feel the warmth of Your presence and the joy of Your love from the very moment they step through these doors. Thank You, Lord, for my home. Use it for Your glory."

We were humbled by such an unselfish act, such a giving attitude.

*Grateful. More than grateful. Honored.* As our guide left us to ourselves, I don't recall my wife and I saying too much to each other. We walked the halls of the apartment. We looked at each old picture on the walls; admiring each antique, marveling at the grace of God. Randee finally went to bed, but I sat in the old rocker in the tiny living room and tried to comprehend the profoundness of the moment and the happenings of this day.

The tick of the grandfather clock in the small entry seemed to lend a sense of reality to this otherwise surreal experience—an opportunity to spend the night in the home of Corrie ten Boom.

*Therefore, as we have opportunity, let us do good to all, especially to those who are of the household of faith.*
(Gal. 6:10)

# ·18·

# I Bumped into the Door

I didn't *feel* like going to church yesterday. In all honesty, I didn't *want* to go to church. The spirit was strong, but the flesh was weak. That doesn't happen often, mind you, but it happened yesterday. I didn't give a moment's thought to *not* going, of course. I'm a pastor and the place for me on Sundays I don't *feel* like going to church . . . is church.

So, I went about my Sunday morning routine of showering and getting dressed and out the front door—all before seven o'clock in the morning—just like I do every Sunday. I put on my "happy face" before I drove into the church parking lot. I didn't tell a soul how I really felt because I've learned something over the years. People just sort of "expect" pastors to *feel* like going to church, and if we walked around telling folks when we didn't feel like going, they might think we were *human* or something.

So I didn't mention the fact that I didn't *feel* like being there to anyone when I arrived. I just got out of my car and walked toward the church. That's when something wonderful happened.

I saw Jesus.

Every Sunday morning for the last six or seven years, Charlie Jones has provided coffee for our church fellowship time before and after our services. He is there early so he can make the coffee before anyone else arrives. He pours that hot black coffee into a large, insulated server and then pushes it on a cart over to our patio area. I've noticed him pushing that coffee cart up the sidewalk of our church every Sunday for years now—every Sunday, whether he felt like it or not. As I watched Charlie push that cart up the sidewalk, I smiled and said hello . . . to Jesus: unselfish, serving, faithful.

As I came through the doors of our church and into the lobby, I noticed Tom and Alice. They're in that same spot every Sunday. Greeters, we call them. An extended hand and a friendly smile are the tools of their ministry. "Good morning, Pastor," they said to me. They are warm and caring people who give their warmth away at the door of the church. Tom doesn't know it, but as he put his arm around my shoulder and asked me how my week went, I felt Jesus caring for me. He walked alongside me for awhile as I made my way across the church lobby and toward my office. As I walked into my office and closed its door behind me, I sensed that I had been with Jesus. Same caring touch; same soft, gentle, understanding voice.

Jesus just sort of followed me around yesterday at church. When Joe McCarron, one of our ushers handed me my bulletin as I walked into the worship center, his acceptance of me, and his genuine expressions of Christ's love made me know I was in the right place and in the presence of Jesus. Such a selfless, simple task, but yesterday, it encouraged me in a way that only Jesus could have known. Yesterday was a day when *this* pastor needed to teach and preach and sing—but he didn't feel like coming. So He stood at the door of the Father's house and waited for me with a bulletin and a word of encouragement.

All day long yesterday, I noticed Him. During the education hour, I walked by the play yard, where the first graders were enjoying their snack and play time before children's worship began. I heard His voice talking to a child as He pushed her in the swing. I heard Him laughing as the little girl asked Him to push her, "Higher, teacher. Higher!" I peeked around the fence and saw Terry Roberts. He's been teaching those little children every Sunday for years and years, holding them on his lap, caring for them, loving them.

I didn't *feel* like going to church yesterday morning and no one knew how low I was . . . until now . . . no one but Jesus. If I'd have stayed home I'd have missed the experience of seeing Him at work in His church. But what's even more important is that if Charlie or Tom or Joe had stayed home, yesterday would have been a very difficult day for this pastor.

Just a reminder, then: The next time you don't feel like going to church, make the effort anyway. There may just be a visitor or friend or child—or yes, even a pastor—who needs to see Jesus, not when he walks into church . . . but when he bumps into the Church as he reaches for the Door.

> *Let us not give up meeting together,*
> *as some are in the habit of doing,*
> *but let us encourage one another—*
> *and all the more as you see the Day approaching.*
> (Heb. 10:25 NIV)

# ·19·

# The Christmas Card

He would be glad when the Christmas season was over. So many activities and parties and being away from his wife had made him weary of " 'Tis the season to be jolly." He left his office to go home a few minutes early on Friday evening. Nearly sixty hours of hard work that week had meant he hadn't seen his pregnant wife in several days except for a short hello, a quick kiss, and out the door.

When he arrived home, his wife was not in the living room as usual. He quietly slipped through the house, supposing she might be asleep or resting. As he cracked the door to the bedroom of their small apartment, he saw his wife sitting on the edge of the bed, tearful red eyes, and a red nose to match. He knocked gently and sat down beside her on the bed, asking her what was the matter.

"It's the baby. I'm going to have a baby in less than two months, and we have no money. We have no medical insurance and no way to pay the doctor. Your salary doesn't even begin to pay the bills, and I'm worried." He had known she was worried before, but now, as she sat on the bed next to him, his husband-heart turned to mush at the sight of her tears.

He tried to encourage her with words like, "God will help us." She was a strong Christian and had been a believer since her childhood. But she was also pregnant and about to deliver their first child. Feeling the baby kick within reminded her—daily, minute-by-minute—that the moment was coming and nearly upon them when a baby would enter their world.

How would they pay for this baby?

The man wanted very much to comfort and assure his wife. He held her in his arms for awhile and then began to pray. "Lord, I thank You for my wife. She is a wonderful gift from You and she is afraid. I am too, Lord. We have a baby coming in a few weeks, now, and we can't see any way we'll be able to pay the hospital bill. We are afraid because we can't see. We can't see tomorrow, and it makes us afraid. We've never had a baby before, and that makes us afraid. We believe You and Your Word, Your promise that You won't leave us alone. We believe it, Lord. *I* believe it . . . but I can't *see* it.

"Never in my entire life have I ever asked You for a sign, Lord; I'm not even sure I believe in asking for signs. But we need a sign from You that everything is under Your control. Forgive our lack of faith, but if You could give us some indication that everything will be okay, I'd sure appreciate it. I can hardly stand to see my wife worry like this."

The prayer the man prayed was simple and ineloquent. He held his wife for a few more moments, and then they changed the subject of their conversation.

That night they attended a Christmas gathering at the home of some friends. During the evening, the hostess of the party gave the couple a card—a Christmas card that had been dropped off at the house earlier in the evening for them. She did not know the man who left the card, but his instructions to her were to deliver it to the young couple. Because of the party atmosphere, and the many people milling around, the young husband took the card and slipped it in his jacket pocket without opening it.

The drive home after the party was cold and foggy, and the young couple were glad this was the final festive gathering of this Christmas season. When they arrived home, they hurried into their small apartment and prepared their weary selves for bed and a coveted night's rest.

As the young couple lay in the darkness, the husband remembered the Christmas card in his jacket pocket. Wondering about its origin, he got out of bed, turned on the light, and walked to his closet. Reaching inside the pocket of his jacket, he removed the card, came back to the bed and sat down next to his wife, who by this time was also curious.

He opened the card, and read its simple message aloud:

*Dear Brother and Sister,*
*Please accept this as a sign from the Lord that everything is*
*going to be fine, and that God has everything under control.*

Tucked inside the envelope with the card was a five-dollar bill. Not five-hundred, nor five-thousand; a five-dollar bill inside a priceless note that was unsigned.

The young couple looked at the card for a long while before they turned out the light and finally went to sleep. But as they drifted off to sleep, they marveled at the happenings of this night. Like Mary of old, they "pondered these things" in their hearts.

Six weeks later, their first child was born. They sat together in the hospital room, the young mother nursing the wonderful gift they had received. Later, the new mother held the baby in her arms as the nurse wheeled her to the door and the waiting car. The proud husband followed along behind.

In his pocket were two pieces of paper. One was a receipt from the hospital for the room charges and delivery fees, marked "paid in full." Money for the birth had been provided from totally unexpected sources over the last six weeks, gifts from family and friends and opportunities for the young man to earn extra wages. The other was a Christmas card, worn and tattered and well-read. God had delivered on two counts: a fine son and a wonderfully-fulfilled promise.

But this is not a story about a baby. It is not a story about a mysterious Christmas card. It is not about asking God for a sign or how to formulate a prayer so that God will give us what we want. It is not a story about how to put out a fleece before God so He will tell us what to do.

It is a true story about His faithfulness; a faithfulness that is absolute and always and forever. The need was not extraordinary. Almost all young couples wonder about how they will pay for their babies. The Christmas card was not extraordinary. The five dollars could have been sent from an anonymous friend wishing to encourage the young couple.

No, the extraordinary element in this story is God Himself—Omniscient, Omnipotent, and the Only Wise God—who longs for us to know that He is watching and caring and counting every tear.

*Can a woman forget her nursing child,*
*And not have compassion on the son of her womb?*
*Surely they may forget,*
*Yet I will not forget you.*
(Isa. 49:15)

# ·20·

# The Duffel Bag

My dad's a helpful sort of guy. He grew up in the hills of Missouri's Ozarks—in the country—where neighbors help each other if they can. He likes people, and I've noticed that even though he's retired now from the construction trade, he still enjoys helping friends and relatives with their little remodeling jobs and fix-it-up projects. He's been that way for as long as I can remember. My dad's the kind of guy who'll go out of his way to let a driver know she left her lights on when she got out of her car on a foggy morning. Honest. Friendly. You'd like my dad if you knew him.

A couple of years ago, I decided to visit my folks for a few days, and I hopped a flight from the San Francisco Bay area to St. Louis. My folks live nearby, on the Illinois side of the Mississippi River. My dad met me at the airport. After a warm hug and handshake, he grabbed my flight bag and we started down the concourse. As we walked along, I told him the story of my flight and the meal and the bumpy weather over Colorado. Then he told me his story about the man he helped . . . and *his* story was much better.

He had arrived at the airport about an hour early so he could get a good parking spot and check on the flight. He walked through the terminal to the flight information display, jotted down the concourse and gate number of my flight, and then caught a quick cup of coffee before making his way down the corridor to wait for my plane. As he walked, he saw a man ahead of him with two large trunks—one in each hand. "I noticed he was having a lot of trouble carrying those heavy trunks," he said. He followed the man, watching him struggle to make his way toward the security check area.

*This guy's gonna be late for his plane if he doesn't get some help*, Dad thought. My dad told me he walked up behind the man and offered to carry the duffel. "You've got more than you can handle here. I'd be glad to give you a hand," he said. The man paused only for a moment, thanking my dad for his offer and accepting at the same time. The man said he was afraid he was going to miss his flight if he didn't hurry, so he'd appreciate the kindness.

My dad lifted the heavy duffel onto his shoulder, and he and the man walked briskly down the corridor. As they arrived at the security check area, the man placed his two trunks on the conveyor to be x-rayed and walked through the metal detector. My dad followed suit with the duffel, placing it on the conveyor and walking through the metal detector to wait for it on the other side.

But something was wrong. The conveyor stopped as the duffel passed into the examination chamber. An alarm sounded. Security police came from everywhere, surrounding my helpful dad. "Man, they swarmed on me like ten tall buildings," Dad said. "They made me put my hands behind my back, and they put handcuffs on me. They frisked me. It was terribly embarrassing, with people standing around staring at me. I felt like a criminal, and I didn't even know what I had done!" He said they ushered him into a room immediately adjacent to the security check area.

Then the questioning started. The pistol. Why'd he have it? "What pistol?" my dad asked. "I don't own a pistol. I wouldn't *have* one of those things. The only thing they're good for is shootin' people, and I'm certainly not interested in that."

Oh, he had a pistol all right, they said. They found it in *his* duffel bag—a loaded pistol. "Loaded pistol?" said my dad. "You mean that guy I helped had a loaded pistol in that bag? I don't even know that man. I just saw him struggling down the hall with more than he could carry. I asked him if I could help. I had no idea he had a gun in that duffel bag."

The man with the luggage soon explained to the authorities that my dad was just trying to help. The police interrogated Dad for more than thirty minutes before they finally said he could leave. "What happened to the guy with the gun in his duffel?" I asked.

"I don't know," replied my dad. "The last time I saw him, the police were taking him away for further questioning." As my dad walked along telling me the story, he laughed. He said he felt like a country boy who had come to the big city and stumbled into a scene out of the Keystone Cops.

But not all stories about country boys who come to the big city are funny. I know one story, in fact, that's not funny at all.

The Bible mentions in the book of Mark that he was a man on his way in from the country. He must have noticed the crowd that had gathered. "A crucifixion," someone must have said. "They're going to crucify a Jew today." Had he come to town to watch them hang the Jew? Did he stand in the front row of the entourage so he'd have a good view? We don't know why he was there. The Bible doesn't say. We only know he was. He must have seen the Roman soldiers with their whips snapping at condemned flesh and watched the blood from the guilty one's back splattering the crowd. Some who watched were no doubt disgusted and repulsed at the brutality. Others were probably indignant that this Jew had the nerve to bleed on them. Down the narrow street toward the country boy they marched; a band of Roman soldiers being led by a trouble-making Jew who struggled to carry His own cross. We don't know what they said. We can only imagine what the captain of the guard might have said.

"Too slow! This Jew is too slow. If we don't pick up the pace, we'll be late." Snap went the whip on the bludgeoned, bleeding back. "Wince, you dying Jew; cry out if you must, but don't slow the pace. Don't stumble again, or there'll be more of the same."

The man from the country must have seen this parade of disgraced flesh. Looking now to the stranger in the front row, the Roman soldier might have pointed his whip and said, "You! You with your arms folded. Come here and help this pitiful excuse for a king. We've got to pick up the pace. Take hold of the cross, and help him carry it. We'll be here all day otherwise."

Ruined. I wonder if this man from the country—Simon of Cyrene, the dad of Alexander and Rufus—thought his perfectly good Friday was ruined because he had to help a total stranger carry His cross? The shame and embarrassment of it all. The country boy was compelled, however; he had no choice but to drag that heavy and cumbersome instrument of death through the streets of the city.

And as Simon carried the cross, he walked alongside the Condemned One—the One heavy with guilt, who struggled toward His appointment with death as if the weight of the world rested on His bleeding back. In tandem, they made their way to the top of the hill. All the way to the pinnacle, all the way to a promontory set against the sky—before finally, the two men were finished with the cross. One of them laid it aside and walked back down the hill. The Other embraced it, and laid Himself down on it . . . and died.

> *Greater love has no one than this,*
> *than to lay down one's life for his friends.*
> (John 15:13)

# ·21·

# In a Minute

I know of a tiny little restaurant in Red Bluff, California, that makes great omelets. My wife and I discovered it one morning as we got off the freeway looking for a place to eat breakfast. But the omelets aren't the only thing we noticed. The walls of the restaurant are peppered with sage and salient sayings written on small cards—diversions that occupy the customers until the food arrives. There must be dozens of those little sayings throughout the restaurant, almost everywhere you look.

But the one I liked best is in the bathroom—the *only* bathroom in the entire restaurant. Someone nailed it on the back of the bathroom door, at eye-level, so that when a person goes inside and turns to shut and lock the door, they can't help but be faced with its unsophisticated truth: "The length of time a minute takes depends on which side of the door you're on."

One bathroom. One door. One sign. And a ton of common sense.

Simeon was only three. He lay small and innocent in his mother's lap as the nurses took his blood pressure and prepared him for surgery. The doctors said it was a simple procedure that would take only a few minutes. They called it a tonsillectomy.

But his mother and I called it "open-tonsil surgery," because we were on a different side of the door than the doctors. We were parents. This was our Simeon—our only youngest son. They tried to calm us and reassure us; they said we should wait in the surgery patient lounge. Someone would come and tell us when it was all over. It wouldn't take long, they said.

But I know how long it took. It took an eternity. I was on the other side of the door, and I don't care if the clock said it took thirty minutes. Ask his mother if you don't believe me: It took an eternity.

♦

We used to travel by car to visit my grandparents who lived about four hours away. I can remember asking my mom and dad after an hour or so, "How much longer? Are we almost there yet?"

My mother's response was typical of parents everywhere: "Not yet. A little while longer."

"In a minute?" I would ask. "Will we be there in a minute?"

"Soon," would be her answer.

But it wasn't soon. It took forever. Drives to see grandma take forever when you're eight and sitting in the backseat fidgeting. Parents are mature; children aren't. And how long it takes to get from "our house" to "grandma's house" is purely a matter of perspective.

♦

Randee says, "Honey, will you take out the garbage?"

I say, as I watch a tremendous catch or throw or goal on television, "Yeah, hon. I'll take it out . . . in a minute."

But on more than one occasion, I have walked into the kitchen, after *a minute,* and I couldn't find the garbage. The reason I couldn't find it was that my wife got tired of walking around it, and took it out herself. The *"in a minute"* a wife waits for, after she has neatly tied a garbage bag and readied it for disposal, is not the same *"in a minute"* a husband experiences as he watches his favorite team on their way to victory.

♦

You may not have thought about it, but the word *minute* is not in the Bible. The word may not be, but the concept is. I saw it this morning in the gospel of Luke, chapter 9. The people followed the Bread of Life and watched as the Lord of the loaves and fishes fed five thousand folks. They followed along behind the Physician, as He healed a boy possessed with demons. Yes, they'd seen quite a bit in the last several days; so much so, in fact, that now they were ready to follow Him anywhere.

They walked, a motley, dotted line that followed Truth. The people who followed Jesus were inspired, enthralled, captivated by the presence of the Master. They would follow this man to the ends of the earth—well, . . . *maybe* they would follow Him to the ends of the earth, depending on how far it was. In the midst of this parade, Jesus issued a peremptory call—simple to understand, impossible to ignore. It demanded a response.

He said, "Follow Me."

A moment of truth. The man next to Jesus mumbled something about needing to bury his father first, but what I think he really meant was, "Right. I'll follow, but give me a minute. I have some personal matters that I need to attend to first. It shouldn't take too long: I'll be with You in a minute."

Another guy in line heard the dialogue, and chimed in, "I'll follow, too, but first I need to go back and say good-bye to my family." He seemed to be saying, "I'll follow You, unless what You mean by that is that I can't keep some reasonable ties with my former life. If that's what You mean, then I'll need a minute."

We don't know who they were. We don't know if their *minute* was ever up. We don't know if they ever buried their dead or said their good-byes. We don't know if they ever followed Jesus after this conversation. The Bible doesn't say.

Jesus didn't say He was sorry. He didn't seem to have any regrets that He had called at an inconvenient time.

Jesus doesn't have to apologize for calling men and women to a place of obedience and sacrifice . . . and immediacy.

He almost seems to be saying, "If you're going to be a follower, then follow Me. Don't try to mix your old life with New Life. Don't look back. Don't take your eyes off the Truth.

Don't *take* a minute or *waste* a minute . . . or *wait* a minute, because minutes have a way of becoming lifetimes, and the length of time a minute takes depends on which side of the Door you're standing on.

*I am the door.*
(John 10:9)

# ·22·

# I Hate It When That Happens

How would you finish this statement: "I hate . . ."?

If your mother was like mine, you learned at a very early age to be careful how you used that word *hate*. Never, for example, would I entertain the thought of inserting a person's name in the blank after *hate*. You don't hate people. People are created in God's image, and to hate someone would be a grievous sin. So I learned not to put people's names in the blank after "*I hate* . . ." (even though I did have an intense dislike for Butchy Sandstrom in second grade, but I didn't mention it to my mother).

Most of the time, it wasn't even permissible for me to hate a particularly distasteful vegetable. I learned as I sat at the table in my growing-up years that food was provided by God, and cooked by my mother, and to intimate that you hated what either of those two sovereigns had set before you was positively unthinkable, to say nothing of unhealthy. I wasn't forced to eat what I didn't like, mind you, but critical commentary on dinner was totally unappreciated at our house and brought with it a certain and immediate invitation to leave the table without finishing—the comment or the meal.

No, you didn't *hate* people, and at least while you were sitting at the dinner table you didn't *hate* vegetables—not out loud, anyway.

It did seem to be permissible to hate other annoyances, however. For example, mosquito *bites* were okay to hate. When I was young, mosquitoes used to eat me up. When I scratched a mosquito bite too much and it became red and sore, I could express my hate as my mother put ointment on the bite. But, I remember my mother's corrective rejoinder if I said, "I hate mosquitoes." She had what seemed to me a peculiar theology about mosquitoes, a sort of circuitous logic that seemed to envelop everything from the tiniest insect to the largest of animals. "Do you know why God made mosquitoes?" she would ask.

I hated it when she asked me questions I didn't have a good answer for.

"Well," she would say, "God made mosquitoes so the frogs would have something to eat. If there were no mosquitoes, the poor little frogs would have nothing to eat."

While I knew better than to argue with my mother, deep inside where she couldn't look, I also knew that her logic must be flawed. If God created one thing so another thing would have something to eat—if God created mosquitoes so frogs would have something to eat—then it seemed to me that the next logical step in that proposed food chain was that *I* was created so that the *mosquitoes* would have something to eat, and that just didn't seem to be right. Intuitively, I knew I had a deeper reason for being than providing nourishment for mosquitoes. I didn't argue, though. I just let it go at hating mosquito bites.

Since I've grown up, I've come to appreciate that there are many things I can "legally" hate. I hate cars. I know very little about how they operate; I know where to put in the gas and the key. About once every other year, I also put in oil. But I hate cars . . . and they hate me. I hate plumbing, too. It leaks, but I can rarely figure out why. I've replaced all of the pipes and fittings under our kitchen sink twice and the plumbing still drips. (Have I mentioned that I *hate* drips?) There are all sorts of things I hate: ball-point pens that skip, flashlights whose supposed ever-ready batteries never are, anything—anything that is late, standing in any line, the sound of a vacuum cleaner.

I typed an invitation for people in our office to write down the things they hate. I won't share all of the results, but here's what some of them said they hated:

- Sushi, Liver (Ugh!), Anchovies, Raw Onions
- Okra (You know . . . the Vegetable) (Obviously, this person never met my mother!)

- Cleaning house (Note: This particular "hate" received more than one vote, but in almost every case the person who hated cleaning house *loved* a clean house. You figure out the significance of that bit of data!)
- Shoes that hurt my feet
- Cold coffee (3 votes)
- Bugs (dead) on my windshield
- Potty training
- People who are perky and bright first thing in the morning (It's not normal.)
- Alarm clocks

And finally, one of my personal favorites—

- Memos I receive reminding me about a meeting . . . that happened yesterday

Several of my friends mentioned that they felt better after having written down what they really hated. I guess I did, too. *Cathartic* best describes the effect this little experiment had on me. "Getting *life* off my chest" you might say.

I don't know for sure if God watched my recent preoccupation with things I hate, but I suspect He did. The reason I think so is that this morning, I found a list on my desk of some things He hated. Leaky faucets didn't make His list. Neither did cars that won't run or pens that don't write. In fact, as I read His list and compared it to my list of silly annoyances, I was convinced that I have a lot more important things than

mosquitoes to worry about that may be eating me up.
How about you?

> *These six things the LORD hates,*
> *Yes, seven are an abomination to Him:*
> *A proud look,*
> *A lying tongue,*
> *Hands that shed innocent blood,*
> *A heart that devises wicked plans,*
> *Feet that are swift in running to evil,*
> *A false witness who speaks lies,*
> *And one who sows discord among brethren.*
> (Prov. 6:16–19)

# ◆23◆

# Benjamin

**O**nce an editor asked me if I usually wrote about people I had actually met and things I had actually seen . . . and I said, "Yes."

And he said, "Oh. Well, I was just wondering because if you only write about people you have actually met and things you have actually seen, then sooner or later, you will run out of interesting things to write."

And I said, "That depends."

And he said, "Oh?"

And I said, "That depends on who you meet . . . and what you see when you meet them."

And he said . . . "Oh."

◆

Last week the copier in my office broke down, and I desperately needed some copies of a report. I walked out of the church offices and across campus into the Christian school office to see if I might use that copier.

The office was a hive of activity; school would begin in just a few days. A steady stream of teachers walked into and out of the office. They were already preparing lesson plans and bulletin boards, readying their classrooms for the noise of new students fresh from a summer of relaxation. There were two lines of people in that room. One was a line of teachers standing in front of the copy machine. The other was a line of parents of new students to the school waiting their turn for mandatory interviews with the principal. I watched all of the scurrying. I listened to the secretary answer the phone (which never seemed to stop ringing). And I took my place at the end of the line of teachers waiting to use the copier.

While I waited, I poured myself a cup of stale coffee from the nearby pot and struck up a conversation with a young man who looked to be about ten or so. He stood at the end of a work table and stapled papers. It was apparent that he wanted to do a good job of stapling and collating. I watched him carefully count each set of papers before he stapled them. He stuck his tongue out and moved it from side to side as he worked—an obvious aid to his counting. The cowlick in the back of his blond head stuck straight up (as cowlicks are supposed to) and beckoned me to speak to this helper so intent on doing a good job.

I left my place in the line for a moment, and walked toward him to introduce myself. "I'm Ken," I said as I extended my hand for a shake. He looked somewhat surprised that an adult would be interested in talking to him, but he sheepishly shook my hand.

"Hi," he said. "I'm Benjamin." He looked me in the eye when he spoke, and I returned the honor by addressing him.

"Pleased to make your acquaintance, Benjamin. How'd your summer go? Did you get to do any swimmin'?" I sat down next to the work table in one of those short chairs made for little people that often show up in a school office. Now my eyes were on his level, and as he stopped his stapling and turned toward me, I could tell a longer conversation was about to begin.

"Yeah," he said. "My neighbor has a pool, and me and my sister go swim there sometimes."

I thought I should let Benjamin know how my summer was going, too. "I haven't been swimmin' all summer," I said. "I've been a little too busy, I guess, but my boys go swimmin'. They love it."

The door to Benjamin's life had cracked open a bit. I had sons. He didn't know them, but now that he knew I had boys, he seemed to want to talk about them. "How many boys do you have?" he asked, as he left his stack of stapled papers and walked over to where I was.

"Three. I have three sons," I replied.

"Any girls?" he asked.

"No," I said. "The only girl in our family is the momma, and we try to take real good care of her."

I was enjoying my conversation with my new friend, Benjamin, but the now-free copy machine told me it was time to start copying my report. I excused myself and moved to the copy machine. Out of the corner of my eye, however, I noticed Benjamin still looking at me. As I worked, he watched. He studied me and watched for an opportunity to say something else. When I had finished my stacking and collating, just before I turned to leave, Benjamin spoke again. But this time, there was an earnest quality in his voice, as if he wanted to talk about something more serious than sisters or swimming.

"Know what?" he asked.

I stopped my leaving the room. I turned to face this young boy, and I listened. "No. Tell me, Benjamin. What?" Then he told me, softly as if he were telling me a secret, a disclosure that he must have thought I needed to know.

"I'm suppose to be in the fourth grade, but I'm only in second." As he finished his sentence, he looked away, trying to seem nonchalant. But there was a quality to his little voice that indicated otherwise; a disappointment or confusion or hurt that was easy to notice, but difficult to put my finger on.

I interrupted my routine, and sat back down in the little green chair next to the table where he worked. "Who told you you're supposed to be in the fourth grade, Benjamin?" I looked into his eyes, and listened; hard, and intent and important was my listening.

"I don't read good. I'm in the slow reading group, and I have been for two times now. That's why. I'm s'pose to be in fourth grade, but I'm only in second. I been practicin' reading, though. Maybe next year I can get in the faster group so I can go on."

While I sipped a stale cup of coffee, a blond-headed, blue-eyed boy stood at the end of a work table and told me what he had learned in school. He told me he didn't measure up. He told me—in ten-year-old, muted, veiled, innocent honesty—that he had already learned that he was someone he wasn't supposed to be, watching life from a place he ought not be. He had already learned to define his identity by how many times he had failed.

All around me, adult-types worked feverishly to get ready for school to start. In just a few days, the students would be here, and classes would begin. But I couldn't wait. I just couldn't wait for school to start. I had to begin to teach Benjamin now.

I didn't get permission from the principal.

I didn't have the blessing of the state Board of Education.

I didn't ask any of the teachers who scurried in and out of the office that day: "Is it all right if I teach Benjamin something? Is it *all right* if I tell Benjamin *he's* all right?"

I just did it.

I sat for the next several minutes and talked and visited with my new friend, and I told him what I thought Jesus would say if He were there. I told Benjamin I thought Jesus was really pleased with the way he had collated and stapled those papers. I told him that if Jesus was there, He would have admired the way he had given up one of his summer vacation days just to come in and help the teachers get ready. I told him that when Jesus walked the earth, He used to love to gather boys and girls around Him. He'd have them come up close and crowd around, and He'd listen to those boys and girls tell Him all about some of the things they really liked to do, stuff like swimming and bike-riding and soccer . . . only different.

And I told Benjamin that I didn't know for sure, but I believed that never once—never once in His entire life—did Jesus ever ask a boy what reading group he was in. Not once did He ever tell a child he didn't read fast enough. Never once in His whole life did He ever hold a boy like Benjamin on His lap and look into his eyes and say, "You're supposed to be someplace else."

> *And He took [the children] up in His arms,*
> *laid His hands on them,*
> *and blessed them.*
> (Mark 10:16)

# ·24·

# Jacob's Well

People don't get pneumonia in the dead of summer, but Jacob was seventy-eight years old, and I guess he hadn't heard that . . . because last summer, without warning and without apparent cause, Jacob got pneumonia. He didn't *know* he had pneumonia. He had just mowed and stacked one hundred bales of hay the week before and thought he may have overdone it a bit. But after nearly a week of what he described as "feelin' puny," he went to a doctor who examined him and announced that Jacob had pneumonia. He went home with his wife of fifty-one years, and tried to follow the doctor's orders. He drank lots of liquids. He took the expensive medicine prescribed. He stayed in bed just like the doctor told him. But he continued to weaken. After seven days of strong medications, Jacob's condition was no better. In fact, it was worse; much worse. He finally told his wife he needed to go to the hospital. "If I don't go to the hospital," he said, "I am afraid I'll die." And so, later that evening, Jacob checked himself into a local hospital . . . and began a battle for his life.

Every day, I would go to his hospital room. I sat in the chair at the end of his bed and I watched. In fact, I've been watching Jacob live his life for more than twenty-five years.

You see, I married one of his daughters and for as long as I have been in this family, I have watched Jacob's life.

I've heard him pray around the table, with folded hands and reverent voice, approaching God as a friend and counselor. I've seen him sit with his wife and read scriptures night after night, and I have admired his dedication to God. Jacob was not a pastor by profession, but he was a Christian, (not the *talkin'* kind . . . the *walkin'* kind, if you know what I mean). And I spent much time when I was around Jacob, listening to his walk with God, watching him live for God. Now, I sat at the foot of his hospital bed watching him die.

His temperature hovered at 101 degrees. A lung specialist struggled to diagnose the strain of pneumonia that sapped Jacob's strength, trying a variety of intravenous medications to combat the infection. Doctors are usually an opaque breed, content to walk into and out of the rooms of their patients with little or no show of concern on their faces. But I could tell. As I sat at the foot of his bed, I could see with every progressive visit that Jacob's doctors were becoming alarmed at his worsening condition. There was a presage about their visits; a portending that their expressions masked. I could see it, and it caused me to fear for Jacob. He shivered uncontrollably, as nurses placed a cooling pad beneath him in an effort to get this life-threatening fever to break its hold on his body. I watched, and I prayed for Jacob as he lay dying.

He was losing ground.

I watched as a stream of concerned relatives and friends passed through his room, praying for him, visiting with him. I saw his wife bathe his fevered brow with loving touches and cool cloths. The fever caused delirium, and I listened as he talked of being in the circus and performing. He spoke of plowing with a team of horses and visiting relatives long-since dead and gone. He became more and more disoriented in the hospital, as medication and fever took turns confusing him, convincing him it was day when it was really night; telling him it was time to eat his breakfast when he hadn't touched his dinner.

On one particular afternoon, when I walked into Jacob's room, two young men stood talking to him. They smiled as they listened to his stories. For a brief time, it seemed, Jacob was himself. He talked with them about their day and what they had planned. He gave them a few chores to look after around his house while he was in the hospital. "Make sure the garden doesn't get too dry," he instructed.

These two were his grandsons, and they loved the old man. They would most certainly do what he had asked. I saw esteem and respect in their faces, as they stood patiently and visited with their grandfather. They seemed to be at ease with this wizened one, and they helped him sip juice through a straw in an attempt to moisten his parched mouth. They stood next to him, young and strong and capable. He lay weak . . . and growing weaker.

After several more moments of talk between the patriarch of the family and two of his grandsons, the young men shook their grandfather's hand and excused themselves, promising to "come again tomorrow." It was quiet in the room as I sat at the foot of the bed reading a newspaper. Jacob looked away, out the nearby window, resting I supposed. But he was not resting. He was thinking . . . about his life . . . and about his death. I know he was, because he told me so.

"If I had my way, that's how I would like to die," he said. I looked up from my paper and begged his pardon, wondering if he was hallucinating again. He repeated his wish. "If I had my way, that's how I would like to die." I did not stand, but folded the newspaper and set it aside. Jacob needed to talk.

"What do you mean?" I asked.

Now, the father of my wife spoke without delirium or confusion of thought. He knew exactly what he wished for, and he explained it with a solemn eloquence.

"If I had my way, I would die like my namesake in the Bible. Jacob gathered his children around him as he spent his last breath and blessed them, one by one. If I had my way, that's how I would like to die." Tears welled in the eyes of the Jacob who lay in the bed, and for several more moments we talked of family and blessings and God. I will not tell you all that we spoke, because some things are meant to be hidden in the heart.

But I will tell you that Jacob did not receive his wish.

There was no opportunity for Jacob to gather his children around his deathbed . . . because there *was* no deathbed. Jacob did not die. After eight more days in the hospital, he went home, weak but on the mend. And he was a man on a mission . . . a mission of blessing.

In the ensuing days since his hospitalization, Jacob has been very busy. One by one, he has approached his children. On sunny days, away from sickness and medicine and machines, he has approached his progeny . . . and like Jacob of old, he blessed them. He didn't wait until it was time for him to die. He jumped the gun on death. He gave something only he could give; he decided to model something important for those most important to him. Jacob blessed his children. He sat down with them and spoke with them. He looked straight into their eyes on ordinary days and told them what he wanted them to know. He gave them what he wanted them to have.

When I was a young man preparing to leave home, one of the things my dad gave me as a parting pearl of wisdom was the fact that fathers-in-law could be a wonderful treasure. He said, "When you marry, learn to appreciate the parents of your wife, because they can be a great source of wisdom and encouragement and blessing to you along life's way."

My dads—both of them—are very wise men indeed.

> *. . . and this is what their father said to them
> when he blessed them, giving each the
> blessing appropriate to him.*
> (Gen. 49:28 NIV)

# ◆25◆

# The White House

The small-framed woman scurried up the walk toward the white frame house carrying her nursing bag. A cold wind reminded her to hurry; the weatherman predicted snow by evening. As a home-care nurse, she worked long hours, difficult hours, filled with beds that needed to be changed, oxygen tanks that needed checking, and heavy patients that needed to be lifted into and out of baths. As she approached the gray, freshly painted steps, she double-checked the address to make certain: 3212 Sycamore.

3212 Sycamore was the home of Mr. and Mrs. Sanders. Mrs. Sanders suffered from emphysema and would be the woman's new patient. She rang the doorbell and could hear the voice of a man inside the house making his way to the front door. An elderly man greeted her.

"Hello, I'm Mary Lou from Homecare Specialists. Are you Mr. Sanders?" she said.

The man smiled and nodded his head in acknowledgment of her question. He ushered Mary Lou into a small, cluttered living room and introduced her to his wife, who was sitting on a dingy couch next to a tank of oxygen. The two women greeted each other, and after a few remarks about the biting wind and an "I think it's going to snow" comment, Mary Lou took out her small clipboard and began the initial interview.

She asked about any medication Mrs. Sanders might be taking. Did she have any special dietary needs? Were there any allergies? Did Mrs. Sanders use a walker or cane? What about bathing? Did she need assistance getting into or out of the shower?

They continued the question and answer segment of the interview for several more minutes, before Mary Lou finally looked at her new patient and said, "All right, Mrs. Sanders. Enough talk. Where's the bathroom? Let's wash your hair and get you prettied-up. Would you like that?"

Mrs. Sanders smiled and nodded, but she looked to her husband, who stood in the doorway to the hall. "You'll need to clean up the bathroom first," she said to her husband.

"Oh, you don't need to worry about that," said Mary Lou. "We'll make it just fine."

But the elderly man had already turned and walked down the hall, as Mrs. Sanders interrupted with an explanation. "We have two dogs. We didn't want them to disturb us while you were here, so we put them in the bathroom. He'll need to make sure it isn't a mess in there." As the two women continued their casual chatting in the living room, the home-care nurse could hear the voice of the old man down the hall as he scolded the dogs to get back away from the door. He seemed annoyed and was obviously having difficulty getting the dogs to cooperate with his efforts. Within moments, both dogs appeared in the doorway to the living room where the two women sat talking.

They were not large dogs. One was brown, with patches of white on its side, and ears that looked too small for its head. The other was slightly larger, black with just a touch of white at the base of its short, stubby tail. The woman was not alarmed at seeing the dogs. These were obviously the family pets, and she knew that she would have to become familiar with them sooner or later anyway, if she was to care for Mrs. Sanders.

But she had no way of anticipating just *how* familiar she was about to become with the two dogs.

The dogs seemed to scan the room briefly, as if looking for something they didn't see but were convinced was there. When they noticed the home-care nurse sitting in the overstuffed chair, they attacked. Mary Lou recoiled in fright, as the dogs began to bite at her legs, one on one leg and one on the other. "The dogs! Get them away!" she screamed as the vicious attack began.

The man had followed the dogs down the hall, and within moments was grabbing for them, scolding them, trying to get them away from the horrified woman while Mrs. Sanders watched helplessly. But the dogs were too quick for the old man. Like jackals on a hunt, they darted and dashed around his flailing arms and continued lunging and biting the woman.

She tried to protect herself from their relentless assault by kicking at the dogs, but they would not be dissuaded from their rage. They growled and bit her legs as she recoiled in horror. She swung her clipboard violently at them, pleading with the old man to grab the dogs, to take the dogs away, while they continued their precision attack for several more moments. Finally— mercifully—the man caught both the dogs and dragged them, still lunging and trying to get at the bleeding woman, into a back room and closed its door.

The woman made her way to a nearby phone which hung on the wall. Within five minutes or so, paramedics were on the scene, along with police. They rushed the woman to a local hospital where doctors treated her badly mauled legs. One-hundred-twelve stitches and several hours later, Mary Lou went home.

She called me when she got there, to tell me about this awful tragedy. I'm glad she did. It would have been terrible for my mom to go through such a horrifying attack without letting me know. I was angry at the dogs. I was angry at the people who allowed those vicious animals to hurt my mother. But mostly, I was frustrated because I live so far away. Two thousand miles separate my parents and me. I couldn't touch her. I couldn't see her or hug her or let her see my concern and love. I told her over and over again how sorry I was, and how much I appreciated her telling me about her tragedy so I could pray. It would have been unthinkable not to know.

That's why all of us—we who are the household of God—need to stay in touch with one another. Attacks happen every day. They're not usually attacks by vicious dogs, but they are attacks just the same. All around us every day, people suffer awful things. Human beings created in God's very image—people who live in white houses that look innocent on the outside—are wounded and hurt by *life*.

If I didn't know this story, I might pass those hurting people on the street or notice them waiting for a bus . . . or sit next to them in church on Sunday, and not listen for their hurt or their pain or their fear. But I do. I do know this story, and now, so do you.

*Be kind and compassionate to one another.*
(Eph. 4:32 NIV)

# ·26·

# Whose Turn Is It, Anyway?

**I**'m waiting for something to happen today. It's not important that you know what I'm waiting for; only that I'm waiting and I don't particularly enjoy it . . . waiting, I mean. *Waiting* drives me bonkers. When I'm waiting, giant, invisible fingers seem to drum a nervous rhythm across my life, keeping the beat, reminding me how much time is being wasted on *waiting*.

In the last week, I've endured a lot of waiting. I waited in the doctor's office on Thursday. I stood in front of a sign for nearly five minutes—a sign that read, *Please tell the receptionist when you arrive.* I couldn't tell her I had "arrived" because she was talking to someone on the telephone. When she finally did get off the phone, she left me standing in front of that sign for several more minutes, while she went to pull someone's chart back in the catacombs of the inner office. I took a seat in the "waiting room," which was filled with other "waiters," and thumbed through a year-old copy of *Sports Illustrated*.

I waited for half-an-hour beyond my scheduled appointment before the nurse finally called my name. She ushered me rather unceremoniously into the back of the office to an examination room and handed me one of those short gowns. I have shirts with longer tails than those things! She told me to get undressed and said, "The doctor will be with you in a few moments."

*Moments*, of course, can be a long time when they're strung end-to-end and you're a patient sitting half-naked in an examination room. I sat there freezing to death for *fifteen* minute-moments—I kept track—before the doc finally came in, cheery and humming and oblivious to my wait—my long wait—to see him. After he examined me (for all of thirty seconds,) he pronounced me to be in pretty good health, but he wanted to do a couple of tests, just to make sure. I have to *wait* two weeks for the results.

I admit it. I'm not a very patient patient. In fact, over the course of the last few weeks, I've been noticing that I'm not a very patient *anything*. I've struggled with *waiting* as a dad and snapped at my kids when they "made me late." I caught myself biting my lip the other day because my wife made me wait. Even the *pastor*-me has struggled lately, waiting for people in the congregation to carry through with commitments they have made.

I've learned something about myself, though. When I catch myself being intolerant of others, the problem is virtually always mine, not theirs. I need to stop what I'm doing, take a break, and find someone who'll play chess with me, because one of the best remedies for impatience in my life is a rousing game of chess.

♦

I used to play chess with my friend Ramon. He's a missionary in Colombia now, and I don't get to see him very often. We used to sit and play chess and talk about God and family and church by the hour. I don't remember a lot about our conversations, but I do recall one chess match in particular. The fury of the rain outside made me glad we were inside by the fire, relaxed, and warm. Contemplative as we set up the chess board, we made a pot of coffee and settled in for an evening of chess.

I moved first. Then Ramon moved. No conversation. Just staring at the board.

I moved again. Strategize. Plan. Think.

Ramon moved. I moved. Back and forth the battle raged. After about twenty minutes of play, the game slowed. Each move took a little longer. This was serious stuff. We poured over the board, pondering and weighing each move, each alternative. I made one particularly brilliant move that dealt a devastating blow to Ramon's defense, and waited for his response.

I waited five minutes.

I got up from the board and poured myself a cup of coffee.

I waited ten minutes.

The old school clock in my living room ticked away the moments.

Fifteen minutes.

Ramon studied. He worried. I had him. I could tell he was perplexed. He didn't know where to move.

Twenty minutes.

I decided to rub it in a little. "You want me to help you figure out a good move?" I asked, as I smiled in self-confidence.

That's when he embarrassed me.

He looked up from his concentration of the board, slowly shaking his head. He had an incredulous look on his face, a look I've seen many times on the faces of people who make me wait, an expression that people get when they can't believe what they've just heard.

"It's not my move," he said. "Have you been waiting on me all this time? I moved while you were pouring your coffee. Didn't you notice?"

No, I hadn't noticed. Dumb. I felt really dumb. I'd been waiting for *him* to move for nearly twenty minutes . . . when it had been *my* move all along.

♦

Lord, as I sit waiting for You to do something—as I sit for long hours looking into the board of my life, bored to tears and wondering when people or events or circumstances will move out of the way so I can proceed—I wonder if it's time. I probably should have done it sooner, but at the risk of asking a ridiculous question, Lord: Am I waiting on You . . . or are You waiting on me? Whose move is it, Lord, mine or Yours? In my hurry to be a patient dad and a patient husband and a patient pastor . . . I keep losing track. I really want to be like You. In fact, I can hardly wait. That's one of my big problems. I know You are the Great Physician—and You know how hard it is for me to sit in the doctor's office. Help me today, Lord, to understand that sometimes when testings come, I have to wait awhile to see the results.

*I wait for the LORD, my soul waits,*
*And in His word I do hope.*
(Ps. 130:5)

# ·27·

# Orange Suds

I was raised in Granite City, Illinois, a steel town across the Mississippi River from St. Louis. When I was a kid my folks decided to build a two-room addition on the back of our house for our growing family. One of those rooms was a dining room, and the other was a bedroom for my brother and me. Our bedroom had a gray tile floor and gray walls. I don't remember one single picture on any of those gray walls. We may have had some, but I don't remember them.

What I do remember is the heat. When summer comes to the Midwest—and in Granite City it seemed to me like it was almost always summer—hot, humid air hangs over the town. You can smell the humidity; the air drips with it.

We didn't have air conditioning when I was a kid. My brother and I suffered in our gray bedroom at the back of the house. The heat and humidity were terrible. I remember lying awake at night, my head craned toward the window, desperately trying to feel a breeze that wasn't there. I remember waking in the morning wet from my own sweat, a fitful night behind me, and a day filled with more sweat ahead of me.

Sometimes Richard Justice would knock on my back window very early in the morning. He lived across the street, and he didn't have any air conditioning either. When he couldn't sleep because of the heat, sometimes he'd come over and peck on my window. We'd go out in the backyard to shoot marbles at six-thirty in the morning.

If my mom wasn't lookin', (and she was almost always lookin') after Richard and I finished our game, I'd sneak across the street and eat breakfast with the Justice gang. If I remember right, they had thirteen kids. Mrs. Justice didn't seem to notice how many kids were lined up to get a fried egg sandwich with mustard on it. As I went up the back steps of their house, I could smell those sandwiches cooking. I could see Mrs. Justice standing at the stove handing out those sandwiches. I couldn't resist. When she asked me if I wanted some breakfast, I always said yes. She never told me to go home to eat—not once in all the years I was growing up. Mrs. Justice was a great mom. She had a lot of kids. And she had a lot of courage and character . . . and love.

In the middle of long summer afternoons, I would often go next door to the Marlers'. They were our best friends, but I don't think it had much to do with their air conditioning, well, some maybe, but not much. (Yeah, right.) The air inside their house smelled different from our air. Our air wasn't conditioned; it was raw, wet and miserable air. The Marlers' air was cool and comfortable, and I almost never wanted to go back home. But when it was time for supper, my mom would send my little sister after me and tell me the pork chops were almost done, and I had to come home and set the table. As I left the Marlers' to come back home, and the heat and humidity smacked me in the face, I remember saying to myself more than once, *One of these days I'm gonna get a house . . . and it's gonna be air conditioned.* That's what I said, when I was growing up.

---

♦

## **Nobody wants to live on a klutzy street . . . I'd have given anything to live on a street like Sleepy Hollow Way, or Clayborn Ridge Road.**

♦

---

When I was a kid, I lived at 3019 Myrtle Avenue. The street next to mine was Buxton, which wasn't much better than Myrtle, but it was somewhat better. I was embarrassed about the name of my street. Myrtle sounded like the name of a klutzy television character to me, and when I started school and kids asked me where I lived, some of them laughed when I told them.

"Myrtle?" some of them would say. "You live on Myrtle?" And I would flinch inside. I didn't let them see it, of course, but that hurt. Nobody wants to live on a klutzy street. You know what I mean? Some of my friends had such great sounding streets, names like Cheshire and Carlton and Ridgecrest Court and such. I'd have given anything to live on a street like Sleepy Hollow Way or Clayborn Ridge Road. But Myrtle—3019 Myrtle Avenue—that was as good as it got. And I remember thinking to myself, *One of these days I'm gonna move away from Myrtle Avenue and get me a better sounding street to live on.*

When I was growing up, the summer rain would sometimes flood our street. We didn't have curbs or gutters on Myrtle Avenue, so the water ran to the end of the street and flowed into the storm drain down there.

Richard Justice got to wade in the water and put on shorts and just sit out in the rain. My mom never let me do that. She was afraid of polio I think. She'd try to scare my brother Dan and me with talk about polio and iron lungs, but it didn't work. I could see all the Justice kids every time it rained, and none of them had to sleep in an iron lung. I'd sit in the fork of the double-trunked sycamore tree in front of our house and watch as all the Justice kids got to swim in the rainwater. Lucky dogs. They got an egg sandwich with mustard on it for breakfast and could sit out in the rain all afternoon, too. Not me. But I said to myself, *If I ever have any kids, and it rains and the streets are flooded, I'm gonna let 'em put on their old shorts, take off their shoes, go outside, and sit in muddy rainwater all they want.*

When I was growing up, I never got a pair of black boots like all the other guys either. We called them "engineer boots." I'm not sure why, but that's what we called them. And I wanted some. What I got was a pair of brown, two-buckles-at-the-top, ugly, absolutely nerdy combat boots.

Ron Yates had engineer boots. He was the most popular kid in the class. He was also the best athlete in the class, the quarterback during recess, and my best friend.

We always played football at recess. As we bent over in the huddle, Ron would tell me to go down on the right and then cut across the middle for a pass. And the whole time he was tellin' me that, I'd be looking down at my brown, two-buckles-at-the-top, ugly, absolutely nerdy combat boots and I knew . . . I knew I was going to miss that pass. Nobody can catch a pass in combat boots. I remember saying to myself, *One of these days I'm gonna get me some of those engineer boots.*

When I was growing up, doing the dishes was the blight of my life. My mom wasn't careful at all. She thought nothing of dirtying two or three pans every time we had dinner. When she fried pork chops, the crusty brown stuff on the skillet was almost impossible to get off. She'd walk by and say, "Keep scrubbin'. It'll come clean with some work." I don't suppose it was child abuse for her to make me work like that, but at the time it seemed pretty abusive. I just couldn't understand why she'd cook the corn in one pot and the green beans in a different one. They were both vegetables. Why couldn't she cook 'em together, and save the labor of washing one pot? It didn't make sense to me.

When we had spaghetti—and we had spaghetti a lot—I hated the way the sauce turned the soap suds orange in the sink. I hated the way the water ran out of bubbles before I ran out of dishes. I didn't like the way the dishwater got cold before I was finished with all the washing. And I didn't like the way my brother Dan dried the dishes, either. He always left them a little wet. And I hated the way my sister—the littlest—never seemed to have to do the dishes as much as Dan and me. Why couldn't we eat off paper plates? Why couldn't we be richer and have an automatic dishwasher? Or at least, why couldn't we have air conditioning so that if I had to do the dishes—the yuckiest, nastiest thing I could ever have to do—at least I could be cool while I was doing them? I still remember standing at the kitchen sink at 3019 Myrtle Avenue saying to myself, *If I ever have any kids I'm never gonna make 'em do the dishes, as long as they live.*

When I was a kid growing up, one of the things I wished for most was to *not* be a kid growing up. It took too long to grow up. I was sure life was meant to be more than humidity and dishes and orange suds in the kitchen sink. I didn't get to have any fun. I never got to sit in the rain, like Richard Justice. I had to live on Myrtle Avenue and wear combat boots.

I noticed that grown-ups like my grandpa never had to do the dishes. And they didn't have to eat their vegetables if they didn't like them, either. And they could stay up as long as they wanted to, and even go buy a house with air conditioning if that's what they wanted. They were adults. They could do whatever they wanted.

Well, I'm grown up now, with three nearly-grown sons. The other night my wife made some wonderful spaghetti, with homemade sauce. After dinner, I said, "I'll take care of the dishes." My sons usually do the dishes, but this particular night, I volunteered. As my wife was helping me to clear the table, I heard myself grumbling about *life* and the particularly frustrating, difficult, challenging day I had experienced. I caught myself griping and whining like some child who's tired and needs to go to bed. I loaded the dishwasher, put in the soap and turned it on. But I still had a few pans to wash, so I filled the sink with water and added the dishwashing liquid. I had almost forgotten what it was like to do the dishes after you've had spaghetti for dinner. Orange suds.

*When I was a child, I spoke as a child,*
*I understood as a child, I thought as a child;*
*but when I became a man, I put away childish things.*
(1 Cor. 13:11)

# ·28·

# Memo to a Mugger

*Date:* April 17
*To:* The man who mugged my son
*From:* Ken Jones
*Subject:* Forgiveness

You don't know me, but I feel as if I know you. I'm the dad of the teenager you mugged last Friday on the streets of San Francisco. In case you've forgotten by now, I'll refresh your memory.

My son was the blonde fifteen-year-old with the video camera. He must have looked like a tourist to you, as he walked down that back street with his friend. He may have *looked* like a tourist, but he wasn't. In fact, he's a native Californian. And every year for the last three years, he and his two brothers have joined several other kids from our church for a trip into the inner city streets during Easter break. They leave the relative safety of the suburbs and spend their vacations working in a rescue mission, feeding the poor, and organizing games and Bible clubs for the children of the streets.

You don't know my son, Simeon, even though you've met him. You don't know him, but if you did, you'd like him. I know you would. Simeon is wholesome, clean-cut, and polite. At fifteen, he's the baby of our family. He's low-keyed and relaxed. He walks slowly, with a casual, airy bounce to his step. He loves pets . . . and people.

Last Friday—Good Friday, I guess it was—Simeon called me from San Francisco. It was one of *those* calls. You know the kind I mean; the kind of call you occasionally get from one of your kids that starts with the words, "Dad, everything turned out all right, but I need to tell you what happened to me today." He told me about you, and what you did.

He said he and his friend were taking a short walk after lunch and decided to get some video footage of their trip. You walked around the corner toward them—you and your large companion. Simeon said you greeted them as you approached.

"How's it goin', man. I'm Alfred," you said. You looked straight into my son's eyes and extended your hand. But your eyes quickly fell from Simeon's face onto the camera he held, didn't they? "That's a neat-lookin' video camera you got there. Could I hold it and look through the lens for a minute?" you said. Sim said he tried not to act scared as he answered you. "I borrowed the camera from a friend. I better hang on to it," my son said.

Simeon described the other man standing there with you—the one with the black Oakland Raiders jacket on. The man didn't have a smile like yours. He looked more menacing, more threatening; a tough guy who left both his hands in his jacket pockets as he spoke. "He wants to see the camera, man. He wants to tell his mom what it's like to look through one of those things," he said.

Again, Simeon refused. My polite, kind, sensitive son stood on a city back street and refused to let you hold the borrowed camera. Sim told me that after a few seconds of verbal back-and-forth, you reached out and took hold of the camera. You yanked it from Simeon's hands, stuck it under your arm, and trotted across that littered city street. He told me what you said, right before you rounded the corner: "You need to be careful in this neighborhood. There's a lotta bad things can happen to a person in this neighborhood."

And so it was that you robbed my son last week. He tried to bring a little bit of light to the darkness of the city. Innocent and caring and a great example of a young man who wants to make a difference—serving meals to the homeless and playing games with the kids on inner-city streets. While Sim was in the midst of serving and loving and caring, you and your friend accosted him. You didn't hurt him—at least not physically. But you mugged him, just the same. On Good Friday, you committed an emotional mugging, an assault on his feelings about himself and his good intentions.

I confess that I was bitter and angry with you when Simeon told me what you had done. You took advantage of his innocence, didn't you? The dad in me resented the way you taunted my son, standing across the street laughing at him, turning your back on his gift of compassion and caring. I was bitter about that. Even though we've never met, I was outraged at you for violating my son, for threatening him, for humiliating him. I wished I had been there. I know I'd have been tempted to tell the Lord, "Wait right here, Lord. I'll be back in a minute. I've gotta go across the street and get that camera." Not very pastorly, I'm afraid. But in all honesty, that's exactly how I felt.

I struggled with my feelings about you for several days. Finally, I asked the Lord to help me get over that anger. I've got enough baggage to have to deal with every day without having to drag around an anger for someone I've never even met.

So I mentioned it to God.

I told Him how it feels to be a dad and have someone take advantage of your kid. I told Him I felt like wringing your neck, and I needed Him to help me get over my anger.

He did.

He brought me to a place of quiet prayer, and then He reminded me of another Father and another Son. I wanted to let you know you're forgiven . . . because of Him.

About three years. That's how long the Son walked the streets and dusty roads of another Tenderloin District. Kind and loving and sensitive to the needs of those around Him, He served thousands of meals in bread lines. He brought healing to those who couldn't afford a doctor. He loved the children of the streets, and they often climbed into His lap and listened to His stories. His only purpose in life was to be an obedient Son.

The Father was very pleased as He watched from heaven. What He saw brought joy to His heart, and for nearly three-and-a-half years, He watched His Son brave the dangers of the city streets. He watched His Son grow and love and give . . . and finally, He watched His Son die. He watched, on one awful Friday about noon, as His Son—the Father's only Son—was mugged and murdered on the streets of the city.

He watched, as His Son stumbled down cobblestone streets, straining under the load He bore. He listened as death and the grave hurled taunts and insults and humiliation upon His kind Child. "We've never seen a life like yours," they said. "We'll kill you," they said. "We'll hang you on a cross so all the world will see your nakedness."

And the Father in heaven stood by and watched it all.

He listened, as the sound of hammer striking nail filled the air. He watched, as pain pierced innocent hands. Blood rolled down that gentle brow; royal blood, red as evening's sun. All of heaven listened as a Father's only Son screamed in isolation and aloneness, "My God, my God, why have You forsaken me?" Bludgeoned and bloodied and barely able to speak, Christ the Innocent spent His dying breath to make a call—one of *those* calls—to the Dad of Heaven—"Father, forgive them, for they do not know what they are doing."

Because of the love of that Father, this father is able to say, "You are forgiven." For if anyone knows how it feels to send a Child to the streets of the city, God does. If any

Father knows what it's like to listen to "one of *those* calls" from a Son, the Father in Heaven knows. And, if anyone knows what it's like to have a Son mugged on Good Friday . . . He knows.

*For God so loved the world that He gave*
*His only begotten Son, that whoever believes in Him*
*should not perish but have everlasting life.*
(John 3:16)

# ·29·

# Yesterday

Yesterday, Randee had a headache, Nathan got a new job, and Simeon could have been shot by a kidnapper. A very interesting day was yesterday. And as I looked back on its happenings, I knew I had to write them down.

♦

I don't know how many I've watched. Probably a couple of thousand or so—commercials about "extra-strength pain relievers" I mean. Relieving pain is a big business in our society. So much stress, people wound tighter than clocks, running and scurrying to catch up with their busy schedules. We all need something on occasion to help us with the normal aches and pains of life.

Our medicine cabinet at home has several varieties of pain relievers . . . but none of them work for Randee. In addition to having chronic pain from degenerative discs in her back, she suffers with migraines. About once every two weeks or so, pain assaults her head with such ferocity that she must go to bed in a dark room, lie very still, and wait for that uninvited guest—that vise-like, gripping pain—to walk slowly through her day.

We rate her headaches, depending on how severe they are, from one to five. A "one" isn't too bad; manageable, I guess you could say. When Randee has a "one," she usually goes about her daily activities without my even noticing she has a headache. But the higher the number, the more debilitating the pain. And yesterday she had a "five."

I stayed home from the office and did my best to help her through the loneliness of yesterday. I frequented her dark room with ice-bags for her head and cold cloths for her face after she vomited. Perhaps one of the most difficult parts of migraines is the indignity they foist upon their victims; the vomiting and fainting and feeling helpless and afraid.

I felt helpless, too. I always do. I cracked ice-chips to help moisten her parched mouth. I held her hand and patted her shoulder. I prayed. God knows, I prayed. But in the final analysis, yesterday was a "five," and there's not a lot a husband can do with a "five" but wait it out, endure it like a hurricane's furious gale, knowing that tomorrow will be better.

While I was home with Randee, the phone rang for Nathan. He's nearly nineteen now, and he's been looking for a job for several weeks. I've watched him walk out the door, dressed for interviews, eager to work. Over the course of the last few months, I've listened to Nathan describe the exchanges he's had with personnel directors and store managers. Sometimes, Nathan struggles to communicate—don't we all?—and I wondered if these people who talked to my son *really* understood what an exceptional person they were dealing with. I wished. Every time he walked out the door in his crisp, clean shirt and freshly pressed slacks I wished I could go along and help him. But of course I never went along. I couldn't. All I could do is wait . . . and listen.

And yesterday, I got to listen to Nathan talk to a man on the phone who hired him for a great job. It's perfect for Nate. He gets to drive around town delivering construction supplies. He'll love it. I know he will. There was a certain air about Nathan as he hung up the phone yesterday; a look of satisfaction and accomplishment. Proud, I guess you could say. Nathan looked proud yesterday when he hung up the phone, because *he* had found a job. Someone wanted *him*—the honest, honorable, hard-working Nathan—to be an employee. The man wanted Nathan to come right down to pick up a hard hat and safety goggles, because he said he needed Nathan to begin work within the next day or two.

I'm glad I was home yesterday to hear that. I'm glad I got to stand alongside Nathan in the bedroom, too. Because I was home, I got to listen to Nathan tell his mother (who lay very still in that very dark room) about his new job. He talked softly as he told her he needed to leave; that he had to go pick up his goggles and hard hat, that he'd be back later.

After Nathan left yesterday, I sat alone in the living room and pondered the day's happenings, sorry about my wife's pain and glad about my son's new job.

But yesterday wasn't through with me . . . not yet.

About an hour after Nathan left, he returned with a question; a question, and a concerned look. "Dad," he said, "Do you know why there are so many police cars around our church? On the way home from my appointment for my job I tried to drive by there and they won't even let me near the place. Someone said there's a guy with a gun running around shooting at people up there."

Our church sits high atop a hill, a beautiful forty-nine acre campus. We have a pre-school, a junior high, and high school on our church grounds and Simeon is a junior at the high school this year. He was at school yesterday—and, evidently, so was some guy with a gun.

As Nathan asked his question and expressed his concern, my mind jumped to thoughts about my youngest son. I looked at the clock. Two-fifteen. I knew where Simeon was at two-fifteen. He was out on the soccer field as a teacher's assistant with thirty or so junior high boys. He was exposed, standing in the middle of a half-acre field with nothing to hide behind if some nut decided to start shooting.

I ran to the phone. I dialed. As fast as I could punch in the number of our church, I dialed and waited. One ring . . . two rings . . . three rings . . . *Come on; come on. Answer the phone. I know one of the seven secretaries must be there.*

*Answer the phone!* Finally. Finally one of the office staff answered the phone and I asked her what was going on. "Yes," she said, "There is a man on our campus with a gun. He's been shooting at the police and they chased him into the hills on the back side of our property, away from buildings . . . and away from people. There are more than fifty police here right now, and they have all of the school children and office personnel safe and inside locked buildings and away from the windows. No one has been hurt, and they're looking for the guy now with a police helicopter."

I talked softly, so as not to alarm my wife in the next room. "Keep me posted here at home," I said. "If you don't call *me* back in a few minutes with an update . . . I'll call *you.*" And I did call back. After what seemed like an eternity in my life, but was ten minutes on the clock, I called again. They had caught the guy. He had been thwarted in an attempt to kidnap two women at a local mall. That's why the police had been chasing him.

The secretary I talked to said, "It was so exciting. After they arrested the man, they put him in a police helicopter and flew him right into the middle of the soccer field and landed. The entire student body cheered as the police took the guy out of the helicopter and put him in a police car and drove away."

When Simeon got home yesterday after soccer practice, I asked him about the day's events. Yes, he said, he was out on the soccer field with the junior high P.E. class when someone ran to warn him and the others to get inside. Simeon told me that moments after all the students ran inside the safety of a nearby building, the man with the gun ran right alongside our soccer field—within fifty feet or so of where my son and thirty-five other young men had just been enjoying a beautiful afternoon.

So close. Yesterday, our community, our church, and our family came so close to a tragedy.

I didn't know. When I got up yesterday, I didn't know that the morning's sun would greet my wife with a "five." I didn't know . . . but there wasn't a thing I could have done about it anyway. I didn't know that yesterday would hold a job for Nathan, either. I had no idea, but it wouldn't have mattered anyway. I was helpless to make it happen. As much as I wanted to, I couldn't *give* Nathan a job; someone else had to do that. I couldn't give Simeon my protection, either. I was helpless. While I sat at home, my youngest son narrowly missed being in the middle of a gun battle between police and a fugitive. I didn't know about it until it was almost over, and even if I had known, there wasn't a thing I could do to help.

I guess you could say that due to circumstances beyond my control, *yesterday* just sort of "happened." When dawn broke yesterday's vial, good and bad and vile things spilled into my life and into the lives of those I love . . . and I spent the entire day out of control.

The more I think about it, the more convinced I am there's not a lot of difference between yesterday . . . and *today*. It's out of my control, too. *Today* unfolds like a road map, a little at a time. Wider and wider it spreads its page. Moment by moment, *today* discloses and reveals its agenda, until at day's end, all of its roads and paths and directions are finally known. Experience tells me that some of *today* will be encouraging. Some of *today* will be difficult. I'll do the best I can with *today*.... I'll believe God, and thank Him for His faithfulness *yesterday*, and I'll trust Him with *tomorrow*.

And *tomorrow?* Tomorrow, I'll get to look back at the difficult, encouraging passages of *today*—this day, the only day there *really* is to live—and reaffirm, in the midst of all of life's uncertainty, the foundation of my faith.

*The LORD is my helper;*
*I will not fear....*
*Jesus Christ is the same yesterday,*
*today,*
*and forever.*
(Heb. 13:6, 8)

# ·30·

# On Days When There Are No Words

I sat one windy afternoon on a bench at Mount Hermon's Conference Center in northern California and talked with a magazine editor about writing and about life as a writer. I needed some perspective, and I thought he could help me get it. As we sat there on that bench in the cool afternoon shade and sipped hot cider, I appreciated his willingness to let me wonder aloud about what it's really like to be a professional writer.

We talked of isolation—the loneliness of writing. Good writing must be done in solitude, away from the noise and glare of people; well-meaning people who ask about how you're doing, about how it's coming along, about "how much longer until it's finished?" We talked about how difficult it is to get anything published, whether it's an article, a devotional piece or a book. Competition is stiff. Writing is very hard work. It's easy to become discouraged, when, after you've made your best pass at a piece, editors (who are paid to be critical) violate your "baby" by having the audacity to suggest that you clarify, simplify, or even leave some of it out all together.

I told my editor friend that at times, I felt very lonely as a writer, that I had serious doubts about my capabilities, that sometimes the fear of rejection strangled what I felt I was trying to say in my writing. He sat patiently and listened as I talked about how it *feels* to be a writer, how it *feels* to face rejection, loneliness, solitude, and doubt in your own capabilities. I already knew that writing meant dealing with those feelings, but it was good to hear someone I trusted, who understood the writing life say, "Writing contains all of those elements. Anyone who wants to write must be willing to face them."

Finally, during the last fifteen minutes or so of our appointment, I asked a gnawing question that I hoped he could answer. What of those days—certain days when a writer goes to his appointed place to write, when he approaches a clean, spotless page or a blank computer screen to begin . . . but nothing happens. Instead of a creative stream flowing from a fountainhead of thoughts and ideas, there is a dry wadi, arid and void of life. There are no words, only a waterless riverbed, a dried-up stream where words once flowed. A dry, parched wind has replaced the breeze of imagination and brought with it a dust of doubt . . . a suffocating fear that the words will never come again; a blowing, blinding dust that burns the eyes of the mind and pollutes creative juices.

What's a person to think when there are no thoughts? What does one say, when it seems there is nothing to *be* said? What happens when the writer can think of nothing to write? In other words, what do you do on days when there *are* no words?

Fortunately for me, the man I was talking with was very wise. He did much listening and nodding. He sat, legs crossed, leaning into my queries with a body language that invited me to open my soul and ask serious, difficult questions. And then, he did not answer. Instead, he asked more questions.

"I don't know," he said. "What do *you* think a person who writes should do on days when there are no words?" I spent the next several minutes trying to describe the routine I use for overcoming those days. He had some great insights, too. He mentioned diet and exercise and taking an occasional break from the rigors of writing. But eventually, we both agreed that there's only one thing for a writer to do on days when there are no words . . . and that is to write.

What do writers write, you may ask? How do they write if there are no words? How do they *say* if there is nothing *to* say? They begin. I begin. I force my fingers to type words and sentences that I tell myself do not necessarily make sense. I am not concerned with syntax; passive verbs and conjunctive phrases will not cause me undue alarm on days when there are no words. I am not so concerned with making sense as I am concerned that I write. There will be other days for sorting out; on other evenings I can examine preferred spellings and paltry punctuations that bring clarity to what I have said. On days when there are no words, I simply write—one letter at a time, one word at a time, one sentence at a time.

Writing and living are very similar activities. Days when there are no words are like days when there is no hope—no ray of sun to bring warmth and comfort; only a gray fog of despair that hides contentment; insipid silence that deadens the spirit.

In your life, what do you do when there are no words? On blank mornings when your feet hit life's cold floor and you have no idea how to cope with the challenge of writing life's script for another day, how do you begin? What do you do when you're driving to work and you can't think of one good reason why? You're grateful for a job, but you already know that the check that comes on Friday won't begin to cover the bills that arrived Monday through Thursday. How do you fill the page of another day, when loneliness and isolation grip you, choking the very *life* out of life; when you can think of no words to begin and there are no words to describe your discouragement and the gnawing fear . . . that the words will never come again.

Take it from one writer to another. There's only one way to deal with days when there are no words. Begin. Force yourself to avoid trying to make sense of things. There will be other moments for that. Believe it because it is true. There will be other days to sort and sift and think.

Right now, you must live this day—the only day there is. Yesterday *was*, and tomorrow *will be*. Only today *is*. So begin.

Walk . . . not by sight, but by faith, one moment at a time, one insecure step at a time. For there is another Author—the Author and Finisher of your faith, who is the same, yesterday and today and forever. He knows the plot of your drama and the plight of your life. He—the Word become flesh—will be your word. There will be another day for making sense of it all. The only way to learn to write is to write. And the only way to live—really live—is to know that He is and that He is a rewarder of those who seek Him . . . especially on days when there are no words.

*And the word of the LORD came again.*
(Zech. 7:8 NIV)

# ·31·

# The Peace of Paper

My friend Rich's quiet, reflective manner makes him a wonderful person to talk to. He gives me the impression he actually thinks before he speaks—a rare thing in humans—and then, when he does speak, his words are distilled, salient and worth listening to. I like to hear him talk. He challenges me to grow. Several months ago, I asked him when we could get together for lunch.

"I don't know. Let me take a look," he said. He reached in his shirt pocket and pulled out an eight-and-a-half by eleven-inch sheet of yellow paper which he unfolded and began to examine. It looked well-worn and covered with notations and hand-drawn lines.

I asked him what it was.

"Oh, this is a little calendar system I've made up for myself to keep track of important details and my schedule for the next four months."

"Four months? You've gotta be kidding me," I said, as I examined his "system" more closely. He had divided the front and back sides of the paper into halves, with each half page representing a month. He divided each month into columns and rows, forming thirty little boxes, each representing one day. They were evenly drawn, symmetrical boxes and all of them had one thing in common—a postage stamp. They were all about the size of a postage stamp.

As I peered over his shoulder examining the piece of paper that represented Rich's calendar for the next four months, I noticed his squished and scrunched handwriting in several of the boxes. "Man, that's tiny writing. You must have to really work at getting everything into a box. How in the world do you get four months of your busy schedule and things you need to do on that one sheet of paper . . . and what happens if you have several things to do on the same day?" I asked.

"Oh, I run into that a lot," he said as he finished writing down our luncheon appointment, folded his paper, and put it back in his shirt pocket. "Yeah, that happens a lot, but I work at disciplining myself to only write down the most *important* things. I don't worry about the rest."

♦

Well, I *do* —worry about the rest of it, I mean. I worry about little pieces of paper with phone numbers on them.

They drive me nuts, and they seem to multiply on my desk. I control those pesky pieces of paper by transferring the information from the little notes into a daily appointment and planning book. The system I use is about two inches thick, with a black vinyl cover, and binder rings on the inside. It doesn't have a handle, but it has a firm grip on me and my life. I carry it with me nearly everywhere I go, because if I don't have it, I feel as if I don't know where *to* go. I write down virtually every detail of my life and ministry in that daily organizer: dates with my wife; what to pick up at the grocery store; ideas for stories; people I need to write letters to; reminder notes to call my mother (she thinks there aren't enough of those!); sermon ideas . . . and all my appointments. They all go into my daily time-manager.

---

**God's perfect plan isn't determined . . . by whether I use a two-inch binder or both sides of a page to keep track of all I'm doing for God. God's plan for me isn't in my black binder.**

---

But ever since seeing my friend Rich several months ago, I've occasionally replayed the tape in my mind of my conversation with him. I remember him standing there looking at an eight-and-a-half by eleven-inch yellow sheet of paper that represents four months of his life; one-hundred-twenty boxes, all of them exceedingly small. He has to make important, sometimes difficult decisions about what to include and what to leave out of every day's events and activities. So do I.

No system will manage my time. I have to do it myself. I decide what's important. Every day of life is tiny. If I allow "extraneous" to take-up too much space, there won't be any room for "important."

Finding the peace of God's perfect plan isn't determined by my busy schedule or by whether I use a two-inch binder or both sides of a page to keep track of all I'm doing for God. God's plan for me isn't in my black binder.

My experience is that Divine appointments are rarely written down and each day's fulfillment must find its origin in Him. Try as I might, I will never squeeze the peace of God onto a piece of paper . . . no matter how small I try to write.

*"For I know the plans I have for you," declares the* LORD *. . .*
*"You will seek me and find me when you seek me*
*with all your heart."*
(Jer. 29:11, 13 NIV)

# The Masked Man

I grew up in a neighborhood that had tar and gravel streets. There was a sidewalk in front of our house, but for the first twelve or thirteen years of my life, we had no curbs or gutters. Once a year, usually late summer or early fall, men driving city maintenance trucks would come by our neighborhood. They brought street-sweeping machines with them and swept off all the old gravel and hauled it away. Then they put a new coat of tar and gravel on our street. They never let children play near where they were working. The danger of the big trucks was too great I guess, and the hot tar they sprayed on the streets was extremely dangerous, too. But after they left—after they had finished all their work with the tar and gravel on our street and moved on to the next street—the kids in my neighborhood would get together to admire the new surface. One of the things that was particularly neat to do was play with the tar.

When tar is hot, of course, it pours like water, and the workmen heated the tar so they could spray it on the surface of the streets. But when the tar cooled, it formed pockets and small puddles around the edges of our sidewalks that looked like black taffy. I remember that I could hardly wait for the workmen to move on down the street to the next block so I could be one of the first kids outside looking for pieces of cooling tar.

The tar was perfect for a lot of things. If you were lucky, you could find a piece the size of a dinner plate. You could mold it into all sorts of shapes, making animals, or rolling it out like a rope and pretending it was a snake. Most of the time, though, the pieces you found were smaller pieces, but they were still perfect for making things.

On one late summer day, I became particularly creative with a small piece of tar I had found and made a mask. It was perfect. It was black, and covered the upper portion of my face and nose. I left holes for my eyes so I could see. I fashioned the mask carefully. Such a great idea; I'd be the only kid in the neighborhood with a mask like this one. I didn't need a string to keep it on. It stuck to my face like it had been molded there. I could hardly wait to see myself. I raced inside my house and checked it out in the mirror. I looked just like *him*—the Lone Ranger, I mean. In my mind, I was totally disguised. I put my cowboy shirt on. I got my hat and my guns on and then . . . I walked outside into the light of my neighborhood. Incredible. I was the envy of every kid on my block, as all my buddies marveled at how much I looked like the Lone Ranger. They said they could hardly tell it was me. We played cowboys and Indians all afternoon. For two or three hours we played. I chose different guys to be Tonto, but I was always the guy with the white horse and the cloud of dust and the hearty "Hi-Ho Silver."

Eventually, though, I got tired of playing. I guess it was about three o'clock or so before I finally went inside for a rest. I carefully placed my tar-mask on my dresser and went into the living room to wait for my parents to come home from work. That's when it started.

As I sat on our old gray vinyl couch watching television, a burning began to sting my face. My cheeks flushed, and the top of my nose began to sting and burn. The longer I sat, the more intense the pain became. Blistered. My face started to blister as the late afternoon wore on. My mother came home from work about four-thirty and found me writhing on the couch in agony. My face had swollen now, and my eyes took on the appearance of two burnt holes in a sheet. She asked me questions. What had I eaten? Had I had anything strange to drink? She said I looked as if I was having an allergic reaction to something.

"No," I told her. Through my grimacing and clenched teeth I assured her I hadn't had anything "different" to eat or drink all afternoon. All I had been doing was playing cowboys and Indians. I remember her nervous glances out the front window, wishing my dad would get home so she could ask him what he thought; so she could ask him what to do about this strange swelling and reddening of my face.

Dads are very wise people, and my dad has worked in construction all my life. He took one look at me when he walked in the front door as I lay on the couch. "Burned," he said. "How did you get burned?" I tried to explain to my dad that I hadn't been burned. I hadn't been around a fire all day long. All I had been doing was playing cowboys and Indians with my friends. He would not be dissuaded. "I know a burn when I see one, and you've been burned. Were you around any creosote today? Were you around any roofers today—anyone getting a new gravel roof?"

"No," I replied.

"Could you have put your face up against a telephone pole that had been treated with creosote?"

"No, Dad," was my honest reply. He sat down next to me. My dad sat down on the old gray vinyl couch, and after he examined my burned face more carefully, he said, "Tell me *exactly* what you've been doing since I left this morning." All I had been doing was playing Lone Ranger, I said. I made a mask, but not with creosote. I just used some tar I found in the street.

"Tar has creosote in it, son," my dad said. "When you put the mask on your face and left it there, the creosote began to burn. There's not a lot to do now but wait for the burn to go away."

After several hours, the sting and agony of the creosote burn did subside . . . but not the memory of it. Over the course of the next ten days or so, every time I looked in the mirror, I saw the outline of a mask, etched by my own peeling and flaking facial skin. In my own reflection, I saw an epidermal reminder of the pain caused by wearing a mask.

I never made another mask out of tar after I was burned. But that's not to say I've never worn another mask. In fact, almost everyone I know puts on a mask now and then. Over the course of my life I've caught myself occasionally playing a role—wearing a mask—pretending I was something or someone I wasn't. I'm not sure I ever fooled anyone, especially God. There isn't a lot of difference between putting on my black mask made of tar and my putting on a mask to hide my insecurities and frailties. Beneath both of them, harm and hurt are the certain result. And because God has never cared for things hidden and "pretend," sooner or later I have to take off my mask. Every time I do, the only person I ever find beneath its pretendings . . . is me.

*And we, who with unveiled faces all reflect the Lord's glory,*
*are being transformed into his likeness*
*with ever-increasing glory, which comes from the Lord,*
*who is the Spirit.*
(2 Cor. 3:18 NIV)

# ·33·

# The Retreat

Last weekend I went to a men's retreat with about fifty other guys. I decided to take a couple of questions along with me; questions I'd ask of these men who had gathered in the redwoods of California's northern coast for a time of retreat and reflection and fellowship. They were simple questions to understand, but difficult to answer for most men, I think . . . at least difficult to answer aloud. So I wrote the questions on paper and gave each man in the group a copy. "I'm working on a book," I said. "I was wondering if you'd like to help me by answering a couple of simple questions. I'd love to read your thoughts, and I'll protect your confidentiality. In fact, you needn't sign your sheet. I'm only interested in your answer to these two questions:

1. Do you experience loneliness? If so, can you describe it for me?
2. What sorts of things are you afraid of?

I read through the responses this morning. The candor and openness with which these men approached my little research project humbled me. The men were vulnerable and honest and transparent. Their stories created an anthology of living; a collection of truthful expressions of how they feel about life's chaos and God's friendship ... and why they really need a Retreat, a Hiding Place, a Friend.

Walk with me in your mind's eye back to a lovely conference ground in northern California; back to a place where nearly fifty men scattered out over a quiet, secluded campus, sitting on benches, laying under beautiful trees, leaned against old stumps, writing secret thoughts. If you could peek over their shoulders, and read some of their expressions—if you could get inside their hearts and listen to them tell their stories, this is some of what you would hear:

*Do I get lonely? Yes—off and on, depending on my relationship with Jesus. My wife and I love each other very much, but our "romance-life" is almost non-existent. If I don't stay in touch with Jesus, I begin to dwell on a female friend of mine. . . . I get lonely for a rich sexual relationship. I talk to my wife about it, and nothing happens. (But I will remain faithful.)*

*I have only recently come to realize that I have been lonely. I've used busyness and activity to cover my feelings of fear and loneliness. A big fear I have is to walk into a room with lots of people and not have anyone speak to me. It magnifies the intense fear of being alone and isolated. I involve myself in acts of responsibility to ensure I am not alone. The tragedy of it all is that I am still lonely, only a very busy lonely person who tries to avoid thinking about it.*

*I get lonely at night in my hotel room and am afraid I'm going to miss something down at the bar.*

*I'm afraid of snakes, and insects, . . . and being rejected. When I was a kid, I was one of the ones you always hear about who got picked last for baseball or football or most athletic games. I know it's crazy, but I still get afraid of not doing well on any kind of team, and I'm a grown man!*

*One of the biggest fears I have is that I will hurt someone . . . so I stay away. I also fear losing my job, losing my health insurance, disgracing my family name, and cheating.*

*Am I ever lonely? Yes, often. In fact, at times my loneliness is severe. I have not told anyone because I do not feel that it would make a difference.*

*Before I really came to know Jesus, I felt most alone when I was around people, especially in large crowds. (Does that seem strange to you?)*

*I call them my "blue times." Every once in awhile I get blue. They never last long, but they do come and stay for a little while. I've had them ever since some of my other single friends started getting married and people look at me and ask, "When will you?" or "Why not you?" The severity is only soul-searching, and not very bad I guess. If you want more info or talk, just call. (Signed, with phone number)*

*Yes, I feel loneliness when I want to communicate with my wife something deeply felt. Usually, she becomes defensive and I feel our understanding grows farther apart. I love her and want to stay together . . . but the loneliness is almost unbearable.*

And one more response . . . a final thought from someone I know rather well.

*Dear God,*

   *I wonder. Does it matter that I feel so bad today?*
   *Does it matter to anyone, but You? Does it matter that I look off into space, wondering what to do next, seeing an airplane flying by, and wishing I were on it?*
   *Does it matter? I wonder.*
   *Does it matter that I can't seem to get the "want-to's" about doing anything at all? Does it matter that when I walk to my closet, I look for something to hide myself with, rather than dress myself with?*
   *Does it matter? I wonder.*

*Does it matter that loneliness and aloneness pervade my
life like a huge black paw? Does it matter that there are days
when I cannot think of one soul who cares—really cares and
is not so preoccupied with their own sorrow and aloneness
and life that they have time or desire to reach out and touch
me?*

*Does it matter? I wonder.*

*Is there anyone else out there who stands, isolated in the
wind; blown, flapping like laundry hanging on a line to dry,
exposed so all the neighbors can drive by and see the private
unmentionables hanging in daylight's exposed light?*

*Where are all the other brave ones who face life's toils
without murmur or mourning or moroseness of spirit? Are
they here? Or there? Am I the only one who is afraid to
mention how afraid I really am?*

*I'm so grateful for that place of rest in You, O Lord; that
meadow of David's "still waters." Away, Lord. Turn my
face away from those skies filled with airplanes on their way
to nowhere. When life raises its voice, threatening me and
frightening me, let me hear over that din Your invitation to
intimacy with You, personal, and open; inviting my spirit to
its solace and seclusion and warmth; inviting my eyes to
read—not a book—but the Book, the Holy Anthology
written by God. Volume of truth, a sound and eternal truth
that gives answers to wonderings and matters, morning by
morning, mourning after mourning.*

*Take me to that place and read to me today, Lord. Yes, read
to me from Your Book, because this morning is difficult, and
lonely . . . and I would be truly afraid if it were not for You.*

*I love You, Jesus,*

Ken

*These things I have spoken to you, that in Me
you may have peace. In the world you will have tribulation;
but be of good cheer, I have overcome the world.    —Jesus*
(John 16:33)

# About the Author

Ken Jones lives in Modesto, California, where he serves as Director of Development and Community Relations for Neighborhood Church. He and his wife, Randee, have three sons: Marcus, a communications major at the University of California, San Diego, and Nathan, and Simeon, who are still living at home.

Jones is a pastor and a frequent speaker at retreats, seminars, and workshops on a variety of topics, including ministry to adult singles, family, parenting, and men's issues. He and his wife have been instrumental in developing support groups for parents of children with learning difficulties, and have also been involved in home schooling.

Jones loves music, writing, reading, and golf.